Date Due	Date Due	Date Due

'Love Took My Hand'

The Spirituality of
George Herbert

PHILIP SHELDRAKE

DARTON·LONGMAN+TODD

First published in 2000 by
Darton, Longman and Todd Ltd
1 Spencer Court
140–142 Wandsworth High Street
London SW18 4JJ

ISBN 0–232–52287–1

A catalogue record for this book is available
from the British Library.

Designed by Sandie Boccacci
Phototypeset in 10/14pt New Baskerville by
Intype London Ltd
Printed and bound in Great Britain by
Page Bros, Norwich, Norfolk.

To the Staff and Ordinands
Westcott House, Cambridge
1992–7

CONTENTS

Preface   ix

1 Herbert and Seventeenth-century Anglicanism   1

2 Bible and Liturgy   17

3 The Image of God in Christ   29

4 'In All Things Thee to See':
   Incarnational Spirituality   43

5 A Sense of Place   57

6 Christian Discipleship and a Holy Life   70

7 Prayer: The Soul in Paraphrase   83

8 A Spirituality of Service   95

   Conclusion: George Herbert Today   109

   Further Reading   116

PREFACE

My motive for writing this brief portrait of George Herbert's spirituality is simply to share a personal enthusiasm with a wider readership. In other words, it is not intended to be a scholarly work but an introduction to Herbert's spiritual wisdom. I have given copious references to Herbert's own writings within the text but in order to make the book as accessible as possible I have excluded scholarly notes. For those people who would like to study Herbert more deeply there are suggestions for Further Reading at the end of the book.

I first read George Herbert's poetic collection *The Temple* twenty years ago and immediately fell in love with it. I then took a copy to India during a nine-month stay and became aware on a personal level of the riches of Anglican spirituality. As a Roman Catholic with an Anglican parent, I found myself engaging seriously for the first time with a part of my own family heritage. I subsequently read *The Country Parson* and began studying scholarly literature while teaching at Heythrop College, University of London, and subsequently at Cambridge.

In writing this book I have obviously crossed two boundaries. First of all I have studied Herbert from the point of view of a historian and theologian but I am not a scholar of English literature. Secondly, I necessarily approach the Anglican tradition as a sympathetic outsider. I take some consolation from the fact that scholarly and religious boundaries are no longer hard ones. So a theological approach to a writer such as Herbert has its own validity. Equally, in an ecumenical age, spiritual or theological traditions that were once enclosed find themselves in dialogue with people from different Christian communities and beyond. The results of these encounters are often immensely fruitful.

I am grateful to a number of people along the way for nurturing my enthusiasm for George Herbert. Mark Santer began the process by lending me his copy of the poetry. David Lonsdale co-taught Herbert with me at London University. Graduate students there, in Cambridge and at the University of Notre Dame have all contributed to a growing appreciation of Herbert over the years. Sister Judith of Ham Common shared her enthusiasm and insights at various times. Peter Fisher read an earlier essay I wrote about Herbert and the Anglican tradition and made helpful suggestions. Mark Pryce recently allowed me to read a stimulating paper he had given on George Herbert's gender assumptions. Jeremy Davies kindly pointed out some omissions and errors in my manuscript. Jane Gledhill also read the text as a literary scholar and offered helpful insights and comments. To all of these I want to offer my thanks while taking full responsibility for my approach to the subject and for the views expressed.

Finally, there are two special debts that I wish to acknowledge. The first is to Susie who persuaded me to turn my enthusiasm for George Herbert into a book and who continually pestered me whenever the manuscript was shelved and more pressing work took over. The second is to fellow staff and the ordinands at Westcott House, Cambridge with whom I shared five challenging and happy years. Their friendship, as well as the classes and worship we shared, taught me more than any book about the riches and variety of the Anglican tradition and what it means in practice to try to live within it. I dedicate this little book to them with gratitude.

PHILIP SHELDRAKE
Salisbury, 1999

1

Herbert and Seventeenth-century Anglicanism

George Herbert (1593–1633) was a complex person who led a varied life before he finally settled down as a country parish priest for a short period prior to his death. This very complexity, and the inner tensions that it undoubtedly produced, resulted in some memorable writing and a rich spirituality. The chapters that follow attempt to sketch some of the themes that stand out as most important: Herbert's deep biblical and liturgical roots; his Christ-centred spirituality; his emphasis on the importance of 'the ordinary' and everyday; his strong sense of place; his understanding of discipleship; his approach to prayer and, finally, his spirituality of service.

Nowadays, Herbert is considered one of the greatest English poets as well as a significant, if less imaginative, writer of prose. Two of his works have achieved a special status. The first is the collection of poems known as *The Temple* and the other is his treatise on the life of a priest known as *The Country Parson*.

The writings of George Herbert also mark him out as one of the major figures in the emergence of a distinctive Anglican spirituality during the seventeenth century. He was a friend of other important spiritual figures of the period such as Bishop Lancelot Andrewes and Nicholas Ferrar, the founder of the Little Gidding community, to whom Herbert bequeathed his writings.

1

Several of Herbert's poems have become well-known hymns that have achieved ecumenical popularity. The profundity of the poetry also inspired the composer Ralph Vaughan Williams to set several poems to music as the *Five Mystical Songs*. To many people Herbert is an uncanonised saint, perhaps a mystic. His impact spans the centuries. Several of his poems appear in the Roman Catholic Divine Office. They even influenced such a religiously unconventional figure as Simone Weil. Just before the Second World War, she spent Easter at the abbey of Solesmes where she was introduced to Herbert's poetry by a young English visitor. As with so many other people, the poem 'Love' had a special impact on her. Simone Weil used it regularly for meditation and the poem seems to have been the medium for a powerful mystical experience of the presence of Christ. George Herbert's spiritual influence lives on and his burial place before the altar of Bemerton village church, just outside Salisbury, still attracts a scattering of pilgrims.

Herbert's Life

Before we reflect on George Herbert's spirituality, it is important to understand something of his context. This context was both Herbert's own background and life and the situation of the Church of England in the early part of the seventeenth century.

George Herbert was born in 1593 into the aristocratic and powerful Pembroke family. He had an illustrious academic record as a pupil at Westminster School and then at Trinity College, Cambridge where he eventually became a Fellow in 1614. Herbert seemed destined for a significant academic and public career. He became Public Orator of the University (1620) and then Member of Parliament for Monmouth (1624). The reasons why Herbert changed his course and settled on ordination may be guessed at but are not available to us in any explicit way.

George Herbert appears to have begun the study of Divinity as early as 1616. Yet he only chose to be ordained as a deacon in the aftermath of the 1624 Parliament. At that point his ordination was hastily arranged with a special dispensation from the Archbishop of Canterbury. Once again the expected pattern was delayed. Although by 1626 Herbert had been made a (non-resident) canon of Lincoln Cathedral and given the living of Leighton Bromswold in Huntingdonshire, he was not ordained priest in Salisbury Cathedral until September 1630. By this time he had already taken up residence with his family as rector of the villages of Fugglestone and Bemerton just outside Salisbury. Unlike many aristocratic clergy, Herbert actually chose to live in the Bemerton vicarage alongside his parishioners. His ministry as parish priest lasted less than three years for he died on 1 March 1633. During his brief ministry he appears to have concentrated his energies on the daily round of worship and on pastoral care.

The various delays in Herbert's life pattern make it reasonable to suppose that he went through a period of struggle from 1616–24 and perhaps again after ordination as a deacon. It is possible to hazard a reasonable guess at the causes. First of all it is likely that he was influenced by important external events. I have said that Herbert seems to have had ambitions of a public career. We need to leave behind the image of Herbert as simply a quiet, saintly and humble priest. In reality he had close connections by blood or marriage with several of the most powerful families of the land. It is clear from his writings that Herbert continued to have a highly developed sense of civic community and public duty. This was expressed in loyalty to the local village, the wider Church and to the commonwealth of the nation. Several references in *The Country Parson* underline this concern. 'His children he [the parish priest] first makes Christians, and then commonwealth's-men' (Chapter X). The priest is 'to do his country true and laudable service, when occasion requires' (Chapter XIX). There is also a long section on the duty for all Christians of public service in Chapter XXXII 'The Parson's Surveys'.

The suddenness with which Herbert moved to ordination as deacon in 1624 suggests that there was some connection between his decision and what had taken place in Parliament during his time as an MP. King James I had gained a great deal of support for his attractive image of England as a peaceful country set apart from the almost perpetual religious wars on the Continent. However, the failure of Prince Charles to obtain a Spanish bride, and the supposed affront this offered to the English Crown, led to increasing pressure within Parliament for war with Spain. The Prince's faction appeared to have succeeded when the King dissolved the treaty of peace with Spain. This train of events, and the disappointment it produced, may well have been a factor in Herbert's decision (as well as that of his fellow MP and friend, Nicholas Ferrar) to turn his back on a political career.

Perhaps, in a more personal way, Herbert's struggle also concerned the contrary attractions of a public career and of vocation to the priesthood. It is not too fanciful to interpret elements of Herbert's later struggles as a consequence of the radical change of direction he had taken. Perhaps there are hints of this in one of Herbert's poems about prayer, 'Prayer II'. We may give up all the obvious advantages of worldly security and success yet the human relationship with God does not merely make up for the loss but actually offers more.

> I value prayer so,
> That were I to leave all but one,
> Wealth, fame, endowments, virtues, all should go;
> I and dear prayer would together dwell,
> And quickly gain, for each inch lost, an ell.

Finally, there is much evidence in Herbert's writings to suggest that his struggle also involved a persistent sense of unworthiness in the face of God's love.

The Church of England and the Caroline Divines

The religious context for George Herbert's writings is a period shaped by a varied group of writers known as the 'Caroline Divines'. This title reflects the fact that many of these writers flourished during the reigns of Charles I and Charles II. However, the term 'Caroline' refers rather loosely to a period that began with Richard Hooker's *On the Laws of Ecclesiastical Polity* at the end of Elizabeth's reign and concluded with William Law's *Serious Call to a Devout and Holy Life* which appeared during the reign of George I. The period was marked by a number of critical events. First Archbishop Laud attempted to impose an aesthetic and ritualistic uniformity in worship. Next followed the Civil War, the Commonwealth, the triumph of Puritanism and the temporary dismantling of the Church of England. The restoration of the monarchy and the Established Church in 1660 was not the end of the upheavals for the last Stuart king James II was considered too autocratic and too Catholic and was in turn overthrown in 1689 and replaced by William of Orange and his wife Mary. This divided the Church of England and a number of bishops and clergy resigned and went into exile.

The period was also a time of considerable religious scholarship. The work of Richard Hooker began to be assimilated into the thinking of the Church during Herbert's youth and young adulthood. Herbert's lifetime saw the true beginnings of 'Anglican' theology as something distinct from the strict Calvinism and Presbyterian preferences of the Puritans on the one hand and reformed Roman Catholicism on the other. More than anything, however, the Caroline period was a time of spiritual renewal and of an increase in teaching on personal and common prayer.

As a Church of the Reformation (while not in all respects a reformed Church), the Church of England was unusual in taking an interest in the spiritual development and guidance of individual Christians. The Caroline period produced a large number of writings that, in different ways, offered a pattern for Christian living. Interestingly, many of the writers were bishops. Much of the spiritual teaching was not systematic but appeared in sermons, collections of prayers and devotions and in poetry. Because the liturgy of the Church was so central to the emerging tradition, many of the writings were in practice companion volumes to the *Book of Common Prayer.* There is also some evidence for the influence in England of post-Reformation Roman Catholic writers such as Francis de Sales or Ignatius Loyola as well as pre-Reformation works such as Walter Hilton's spiritual treatise *The Ladder of Perfection* and *The Imitation of Christ* reputedly by Thomas à Kempis. The latter work attracted Catholic-minded people and Puritans alike.

Among the Caroline writers themselves there was a variety of styles. There were pastoral treatises on the Christian life such as Bishop Bayley's *The Practice of Piety*. Bishop Jeremy Taylor's *The Rule and Exercises of Holy Living* linked spirituality closely with ethics. Bishop Joseph Hall drew on late medieval spirituality amongst other sources for his book on prayer, *The Arte of Divine Meditation*. Bishop John Cosin attempted to fill the devotional gap that seemed to be attracting some members of the royal court towards Rome. Cosin's *A Collection of Private Devotions* taught the observance of holy days, ritualised liturgy, sacramental confession and frequent communion. The value of individual confession and spiritual guidance were also touched upon in the writings of Jeremy Taylor and George Herbert. Bishop Lancelot Andrewes, a friend and mentor of Herbert, drew on a wide variety of sources, patristic and medieval, Western and Eastern, in his sermons and his cycle of prayers known as *Preces Privatae*. Cardinal Newman used this little book for his thanksgiving after daily communion until his death. Then there was the poetry and evocative prose not only of Herbert but of John Donne, Henry Vaughan and Thomas Traherne to name but a few. Interestingly, the most mystical of the writers, Herbert, Vaughan and Traherne all had strongly Celtic (specifically Welsh) connections.

Spiritual Emphases

As we shall see in the next chapter, the Bible and the liturgy of the 1559 revision of the *Book of Common Prayer* were the two key foundations of Anglican spirituality in Herbert's time. However, there were several other important characteristics of Caroline spirituality. First, it was strongly Christ-centred. Christ was not only the privileged revelation of God and the means of God's saving action. Christ was also the explicit pattern of Christian living. There was a special but not exclusive emphasis on the Passion of Christ in a number of writers. In some cases this underpinned a sense that God's just anger with human sin was held at bay by Christ taking upon himself the guilty verdict delivered against humanity. There are some hints of this in Herbert but his predominant image is not of God's justice but of God's love revealed in Christ.

Other important themes were those of creation and the incarnation. Some aspects of Calvinist doctrine were taken for granted in the Church of England. However, most 'Caroline' writers opposed the rejection of material reality and earthly concerns that characterised both more extreme Calvinists and Roman Catholic Jansenists on the Continent. Christian Humanism inspired by such people as Erasmus, John Colet and Thomas More had played a significant role at various stages of the English Reformation. A residual humanism was certainly present in the seventeenth century and may explain why certain continental Roman Catholic writers such as St Francis de Sales were so popular. Practical service of others was emphasised and prayer was to be focused on earthly as well as heavenly concerns. Although some of the poetry of Herbert and Donne reminds us that this period was preoccupied with sin and death, a note of spiritual joy was very evident as well. A particular joy in God's creation characterises some of the poetry of Henry Vaughan and the *Centuries of Meditation* of Thomas Traherne.

Catholic or Protestant?

One obvious fact that united all the spiritualities of the Reformation period, Protestant or Catholic, is that they were a response to the failures of late medieval theology and devotion. In the later Middle Ages there was widespread anxiety about the worth of human effort in the quest for holiness. In many respects, the early struggles of Martin Luther prior to 1517 are a paradigm of the basic dilemma. He strove to observe the rule of his reformed Augustinian community with great rigour, had a longing to imitate the desert fathers of the early Church and tried to combat his moral scruples with frequent sacramental confession. On a subjective level, these traditional means of asceticism and religious practice failed to assuage his sense of guilt and spiritual inadequacy. More objectively, Luther came to see that even if he was theoretically capable of earning salvation by intense effort, no experience could guarantee whether he was justified or not. God demanded perfection but the problem was that it was impossible for anyone to know whether they had reached it or fallen short. For Luther, the result was a sense of futility and near-despair from which he was liberated by the realisation of justification by faith alone. In a general sense, George Herbert accepted Luther's 'solution'.

There has been some controversy about whether Herbert's writings should be considered essentially 'Protestant' or 'Catholic'. Some scholars have emphasised his place within the predominantly 'Catholic' structure and liturgy of the Church of England, based on a traditional threefold ministry and the Prayer Book. The evidence consists of the medieval allusions in Herbert's works and his undoubtedly liturgical and sacramental spirituality. The 'Catholic' school of interpretation also tends to draw attention to the influences of post-Reformation Roman Catholic spiritual writers on seventeenth-century Anglicans.

Because this interpretation was one-sided, it was inevitably corrected by 'Protestant' revisionism. This standpoint re-emphasised that the Church of England was really a Reformed Church, more Genevan than Lutheran, even if there were con-tinuities with the medieval past. According to this interpretation, Herbert's theology must have been unequivocally Protestant and specifically Calvinist. More recent studies have attempted to mediate between these two poles. Thus, what is implied by the terms 'Catholic' and 'Protestant' is not as mutually exclusive as once thought. Members of the Church of England in Herbert's time, of whatever party, undoubtedly thought of themselves as Protestant. This did not mean that there was no sense of con-tinuity with the pre-Reformation Catholic past. Seventeenth-century Anglicanism (incidentally, not a concept used by Herbert or his contemporaries) had a particularity which tended to be overlooked in the past but which contemporary scholars are more inclined to acknowledge. Apologists for the Church of England believed that their Church mediated between the two 'extremes' of Geneva and Rome.

In Herbert's day, there were undoubtedly some strict Calvinists within the Church of England. Indeed, the religious settlement under Elizabeth I committed the Church as a whole to a Calvinist doctrine of predestination, described as 'full of sweet, pleasant and unspeakable comfort' in Article 17 of the Thirty-Nine Art-icles of Religion. However, the Church of England of the early seventeenth century could not be labelled simply as Calvinist. Even Article 17 is ambiguous about the stricter Calvinist doctrine of double predestination.

George Herbert seems to have been typical of most non-Puritan writers of his time in accepting aspects of Calvinist doctrine while not being a thoroughgoing Calvinist. Herbert's writings appear to argue in a simple way for loyalty to the established liturgy and doctrines of the Church of England. In the context of the times, however, this was a less eirenical and a more contentious position than appears to be the case at first glance. Herbert's Church connections, not least with Ferrar, his involvement in restoring and beautifying church buildings, as well as his defence of priestly blessings, confession, processions, the use of the sign of the cross and, obliquely, of liturgical dress may be interpreted as a counter-blast to Puritanism. There is also some evidence in Herbert's poetic collection *The Temple* of a tension between the classical reformed doctrines of predestination and justification by faith and a sense of human freedom and responsibility. Herbert clearly believed that the Church to which he gave his loyalty made it possible to hold together the Reformation doctrines of grace, redemption and faith with a continued stress on the centrality of liturgy, the value of a sacramental life and the need for personal holiness. These discussions about Herbert's 'Protestantism' or 'Catholicism' cannot be resolved in a simple way in one direction rather than another.

Was Herbert's spirituality influenced by contemporary Roman Catholicism? Because the Church of England retained substantial continuities with its Catholic past it was certainly susceptible to influences from continental spirituality. For example, Ignatian spirituality, sometimes in mediated forms (partly through the writings of Francis de Sales), had a discernible impact on seventeenth-century Anglicans. The degree to which Ignatian approaches to prayer or the spiritual life directly influenced specific figures such as George Herbert has been the subject of much argument in recent years. There are probably no direct connections between Herbert and Ignatius Loyola in contrast to the writings of John Donne where there are some obvious links. In Herbert's poem 'Perirrhanterium' (verse 76) there is a probable allusion to the devotional practice of a daily 'examination of conscience' that is so characteristic of Ignatian spirituality. Yet this does not prove a great deal because similar devotional exercises had become widespread by the early seventeenth century. At best it seems probable that Herbert, like many of his contemporaries, was aware in a general way of elements of Catholic Reformation spirituality but these do not seem to have played a major role in his writings.

Writings: Purpose and Audience

The dating of Herbert's two great works and their precise purpose are also a matter of debate. Both works were published after Herbert's death – the poems in 1633 with a preface by his friend Nicholas Ferrar and the prose treatise as late as 1652. It used to be thought that Herbert wrote both works while parish priest at Bemerton. It is now accepted that, while Herbert probably edited and structured the works there, he wrote a significant number of the poems before 1630. As far as *The Country Parson* is concerned, his remarks in the 1632 preface, 'I have resolved to set down the form and character of a true pastor, that I may have a mark to aim at', suggest that the work was written in anticipation of taking up parochial ministry. There is certainly no real indication that the text is a description of his personal experiences at Bemerton.

Even if the main arguments of *The Country Parson* were largely complete prior to active ministry in Bemerton, the preface is nevertheless dated 1632. This suggests that Herbert did not feel it necessary to change the overall content or tone while he was a parish priest. It also makes it likely that Herbert had a didactic purpose even if present-day readers may feel that his portrait of a parish priest was somewhat idealised. The most obvious conclusion to draw from the preface is that the work was intended to offer a model for others rather than simply to be a private expression of Herbert's own sense of duty. The concluding sentence of the preface runs, 'The Lord prosper the intention to myself and others, who may not despise my poor labours, but add to those points which I have observed, until the book grow to a complete pastoral'. In the context, 'the others' would most likely be fellow ministers or those considering such a calling.

Is the work essentially a description of the priest's duties and a manual for the communication of practical information? Such an approach is too simple. Modern commentators on Herbert's works emphasise the rhetorical style of his surrounding culture and how this shows itself specifically in *The Country Parson* and *The Temple*. The rhetorical style probably originates in the tradition of Renaissance humanism that certainly influenced Herbert and his circle. However, such a style also represented a return to the Bible (especially St Paul) and to the theology of the early Christian era (especially St Augustine). Rhetoric sought to communicate much more than information or argument. Its purpose was to evoke love, feelings and imagination and thus to move the human heart.

The prose treatise is a work of rhetoric in two senses. This style was actually intended to move the writing beyond the pedantic and gives it spiritual depth even though, to contemporary taste,

13

it feels remarkably detached. In the first place the book is meant not simply to *instruct* but to *move* the reader to a deepening sense of call. In the second place the text portrays the priest as a rhetorician. That is, his fundamental task, in what he says, does and lives, is to move his parishioners to deeper faith and to greater involvement in the life of the Christian community.

The poems are also a work of rhetoric. Isaak Walton, the seventeenth-century author of Herbert's life, attributes a message from him to Nicholas Ferrar concerning the collection of poems known as *The Temple*. They are 'a picture of the many spiritual conflicts that have passed betwixt God and my soul before I could subject mine to the will of Jesus my Master: in which service I have now found perfect freedom'. Even if the personal tone of these words is authentic, it is widely agreed that *The Temple*, published in 1633 shortly after Herbert's death, also has a conscious structure as a work of spiritual teaching. In that sense, it appears that the poems are as pastoral in their intention as *The Country Parson*. While I believe that the poems are a genuine expression of Herbert's own experience, their purpose is not essentially autobiographical in our modern sense. That is to say that, like St Augustine's *Confessions*, the author's purpose was not to write essentially *about* himself. For Herbert, as for St Augustine, personal experience or the self is simply a rhetorical source by means of which *God* could be communicated to the reader who would then be led to greater praise.

The poems of *The Temple* are structured into a conscious movement or dynamic. Some scholars explain this in reference to certain assumptions about Herbert's theology. For example, the 164 poems can be seen as a representation of the Christian pilgrimage from 'imputed righteousness' (justification) to holiness (sanctification), which is achieved only after this life. There can be little doubt in the context of Herbert's time that he accepted the classic Protestant understanding of justification by faith. However, the poems are too rich to reduce the complexity of the spiritual struggle expressed in them to a simple theological structure.

The scheme of the poems is closely ordered. They are gathered into a three-part structure, 'The Church Porch', 'The Church' and 'The Church Militant', of which the middle part is the largest. It is also spiritually the richest and the most dynamic. The titles of the three sections correspond to the different meanings of 'Temple' or 'Church'. It is, first of all, a physical building, an architectural space within which God is praised in the liturgy. Some poems employ features of the building as a framework for their teaching ('The Altar', 'The Church Floor', 'The Windows', 'Church Monuments'). In doing this, the poems subtly underline the importance of order and beauty in the Christian life. The 'Temple' is also the Body of Christ, the Christian community. So other poems express the Church's year or liturgical order (for example, 'Evensong', 'Mattins', 'Lent', 'Holy Communion'). Finally, the 'Temple' is the individual human soul, the 'temple of the Holy Spirit'.

This last emphasis points to an important aspect of Herbert's teaching. *The Temple* is clearly meant to communicate to readers something of the Christian spiritual path. Interestingly, it seems that after Herbert's death the poems were put to a variety of instructional uses as spiritual reading alongside the Bible and the official collections of sermons, or as a source of quotations for sermons. Having said this, the poems are not primarily instructional. It is true that there is something fairly didactic and morally exhortative about 'The Church Porch', the first of the three sections of *The Temple*. However, this is not typical of the famous lyrical poems in the extensive central section, 'The Church'. Stylistically, most of the poems are addressed to God and therefore take the form of meditation or intimate conversation. Again, a rhetorical explanation seems appropriate. The poems 'teach' by moving the reader to an affective response and therefore ultimately to a change of life. Precisely because the poems lay bare Herbert's own spiritual life for the sake of other people, they also appear to identify with the problems and aspirations of all Christians. This contrasts with the rather more detached and objective style of *The Country Parson*.

Overall, it would not be valid to describe Herbert's approach to spirituality as didactic in a narrow and pedantic sense. Even if Herbert's prose work is rather assertive and detached, this needs to be read alongside the poetry where the painful realities of inward spiritual struggle haunt the pages. Although *The Country Parson* deserves to be redeemed as a work of spiritual literature, there can be no doubt that it is the poems that make the greater spiritual as well as aesthetic impact on the modern reader.

2
Bible and Liturgy

The foundations of Herbert's spirituality are firmly rooted in the context of seventeenth-century English social and religious values and structures. Although our notion of spirituality at the beginning of the twenty-first century tends to be very personal, if not individualistic, Herbert's vision was quite different. For him, to be human implied that people belonged to a community that was both social (the nation) and spiritual (the Church). One of the most striking characteristics of Herbert's spirituality is that it is so completely rooted in the life of the Church. In turn, the life of the Church community was founded on two equal pillars: the Bible and common worship or liturgy.

The Bible

As a Church of the Reformation, the Church of England set great store on the Bible. Two of the Thirty-Nine Articles of Religion (numbers 6 and 7) refer directly to the role of Scripture and accept the fundamental Reformation principle that 'Holy Scripture containeth all things necessary to salvation'. This emphasis on Scripture had a practical impact on the lives and spirituality of Christians through the greater availability of vernacular Bibles and even more generally through the new liturgy. Thomas Cranmer's reform of the English liturgy in itself exposed worshippers to a greater amount of Scripture (and in English) than had previously been the case. This was particularly true because Cranmer made the daily Offices accessible to lay people rather than limited to clergy or to members of religious orders by reducing their number and simplifying their structure. According to the rubrics for the Offices of Mattins and Evensong, the whole of the Psalter was recited over a month. At the same time, the whole Bible was to be read in the course of a year by means of two substantial readings at every Office, one from the Old Testament and the other from the New Testament. In addition, of course, there were the biblical readings at celebrations of the Holy Communion. On Sundays and Festivals, the reading of Scripture was to be supported by preaching.

Throughout his writings, Herbert shows himself to be a devoted servant of Scripture. In his *The Country Parson* he suggests that at the very heart of the parson's life and ministry lie the sacred Scriptures. These are a primary means of divine inspiration and of spiritual transformation both in the priest's own life and as an instrument of evangelisation. Almost every aspect of Herbert's poetry can be traced directly or indirectly to the Bible. The directness of biblical language and the pointedness of biblical allusion suited Herbert's desire for lucidity rather than artifice in his verse. He drew freely on the overall atmosphere of Scripture as well as on specific biblical allusions or references to lay bare the inner world of human experience and particularly the struggle between God and turbulent emotions of the human heart.

> Such are thy secrets, which my life makes good,
> And comments on thee: for in ev'ry thing
> Thy words do find me out, and parallels bring,
> And in another make me understood.
>
> ('The Holy Scriptures II')

For this reason, Herbert sets a high store on the priest's engagement with Scripture as the fundamental source for life and ministry.

> But the chief and top of his knowledge consists in the book of books, the storehouse and magazine of life and comfort, the holy Scriptures. There he sucks, and lives. In the Scriptures he finds four things; precepts for life, doctrines for knowledge, examples for illustration, and promises for comfort; these he hath digested severally.
>
> (Chapter IV 'The Parson's Knowledge')

It is reasonable to suggest that, in the context of the times, this reflected the 'reformed' sensibilities of the Church of England. At the heart of the parson's knowledge and ministry lie the sacred Scriptures. Herbert believed in the power and potential of preaching and that preaching was fundamentally an exposition of the Scriptures. 'The country parson preacheth constantly, the pulpit is his joy and his throne' (Chapter VII 'The Parson Preaching').

A number of scholars have drawn a quite sharp distinction between Protestant and Catholic styles of meditative engagement with Scripture in Herbert's time. One important element is the relationship between the texts of Scripture (particularly those such as the Psalms that highlight deep emotions) and individual human lives. It has been suggested that the spirituality of the

Catholic Reformation was far less concerned with inner emotions, particularly troublesome ones, than were Protestant styles of meditation. Thus, Herbert's way of relating the Bible to the inner world of his experience, and his portrayal of God dwelling in the human heart, have been contrasted with the approach of Francis de Sales whose works were well known in England in Herbert's time. On this score, Herbert's meditative sensibilities in relation to Scripture were classically Protestant. This statement may well be true but a generalised distinction between Protestant and Catholic meditative approaches is too sharply drawn. To relate the words of Scripture to personal experience and particularly to inner emotional struggles is as characteristic in its own way of Ignatius Loyola in his *Spiritual Exercises* as it is of George Herbert.

Scriptural Influences

Amongst the biblical books, Herbert was apparently particularly fond of the Wisdom literature, the Book of Psalms and the parables in the Gospels. Within the Wisdom books, Herbert's favourite appears to be the Book of Proverbs. This is reflected not only in the production of Herbert's own collection of over a thousand proverbs, *Outlandish Proverbs,* but also in the echoes of the biblical proverbs in the over-lengthy and rather didactic first section of *The Temple* poems, 'The Church Porch'. Having said this, the section does contain some good advice about practical behaviour and morals in the style of the biblical book. A number of the later poems of *The Temple* echo the style of the Gospel parables, especially the famous 'Redemption' and 'Love III'. Indeed, echoes of a parable style may be detected in all of

Herbert's poems that involve some kind of story. The effect, like the parables of the Gospels, is to teach by means of an indirect discourse. This is both a means of engaging the audience with serious issues through the immediacy of narrative and, at the same time, of teasing the audience to think and imagine their way beyond the immediate story to the moral or spiritual point. 'Listen, those who have ears to hear.'

It is generally agreed that the single greatest biblical influence and allusion throughout the poems of *The Temple* is the Book of Psalms. Although Herbert actually wrote only one poetic version of a psalm, Psalm 23, more general echoes of the Psalter reverberate throughout his poetry. At least one other poem, 'Discipline', is effectively a restructuring of another psalm, Psalm 38. This was one of the seven so-called Penitential Psalms that seem to have had a particular attraction for Herbert. George Herbert was especially impressed by the devotional nature of the psalms. They were so obviously suitable for Herbert's purposes as their wide emotional range illustrated the complexities and struggles of the human heart. The psalms seem to have been part of Herbert's life in a number of ways. A relative of his, Sir Philip Sidney, had made his own translation of the psalms. The daily recitation of the whole Psalter was a central discipline of the Little Gidding community led by Herbert's great friend and spiritual confidant, Nicholas Ferrar. The greatest influence of all, of course, was the liturgy of the Church of England where the twofold daily Office, of which Herbert was so fond, exposed him to a regular cycle of psalms. Interestingly, Herbert's references are consistently to the translation of the psalms in the Great Bible of 1539 which was the version used in the liturgy and eventually formally incorporated into the Prayer Book.

Interestingly, when Herbert speaks of the 'knowledge' of

Scripture, what he means bears a striking resemblance to medieval monastic understandings of *lectio divina*, or the meditative–contemplative reading of Scripture. In this understanding, there is almost a sacramental quality to Scripture. The Word of God that has the power to transform human lives is present and accessible in and through the written words.

> Oh Book! infinite sweetness! let my heart
> Suck ev'ry letter, and a honey gain,
> Precious for any grief in any part;
> To clear the breast, to mollify all pain.
>
> ('The Holy Scriptures I')

This applies first of all to the parson's own knowledge. The means of knowledge is the heart which 'sucks' the words of Scripture in order to allow its 'honey' to sweeten, to heal and to enlighten.

> The second means [of understanding] is prayer, which if it be necessary even in temporal things, how much more in things of another world, where the well is deep, and we have nothing of ourselves to draw with? (Chapter IV)

The priest is to approach Scripture always in a spirit of prayer rather than of purely intellectual enquiry.

Liturgy

While many of the seventeenth-century Anglican writers emphasised the discipline of a spiritual life and the practices needed to sustain this, they believed above all that spirituality should be rooted not only in Scripture but also equally in the liturgy of the Church. The *Book of Common Prayer* is fundamental to our understanding of the whole period because it was in corporate worship that spiritual writers such as Herbert found their main inspiration.

The life and spirituality of the Church to which Herbert gave his love and loyalty was based firmly on corporate prayer. The key foundational document of the sixteenth-century reform was not a set of theological treatises or a catechism of belief but the *Book of Common Prayer*. This was at the heart of Herbert's life and teaching. Archbishop Thomas Cranmer's second Prayer Book of 1552 and the 1559 revision familiar to Herbert was not simply a translation and radical reform of the pre-Reformation Sarum Missal. It was also a manual of spiritual teaching intended to inculcate a certain spiritual temperament or attitude of heart and mind. Herbert understood well that, in the Prayer Book, theology and faith were balanced with worship and spirituality, and the sacred was balanced with the secular. The personal side of an individual Christian's spirituality was to be shaped by living and worshipping as part of the people of God, a community that is both ecclesial and civic. The Prayer Book encouraged a rhythmic approach to life – the rhythm of the liturgical year, the monthly recitation of the psalms and the daily twofold Office.

There is an inherent tension in the Anglican approach to spirituality – and not an unfruitful one – between the corporate and the personal dimensions. Of course, this tension is to some extent present in all Christian spiritual traditions but within the history of Anglicanism it is defined in a rather specific way. The key to this lies in the very title of the foundational document. It is a book of *common* prayer. The personal side of spirituality is allowed its importance but within the explicit context of the 'commonwealth' – the people of God. A person never prays alone. Equally the Prayer Book suggests that Christians are not called to exist solely within a gathered, purified community of right believers. This was part of the battle between supporters of the Prayer Book and what we might call 'the Puritan tendency' in Herbert's day. All the common markers of human life are touched upon in the pages of the *Book of Common Prayer* as well as special personal, collective or national needs.

The language and structure of the Prayer Book influenced all seventeenth- and eighteenth-century Anglican literature. Because of this, Anglican spirituality is firmly liturgical. It is based on prescribed texts that came to be cherished rather than on spontaneity. Worship was understood as something determined by the Church rather than as something subjective and experiential. Worship according to the Prayer Book was also intended to be a means of unity. The same texts were to be used everywhere and by everyone whatever their personal theological positions or spiritual temperament.

It was significant for the emergence of a more coherent 'Anglican spirituality' that the Church retained many of the traditional pre-Reformation structures such as saints' days, the cycle of the liturgical year and the rhythm of the liturgical day and week. However, there was a new stipulation that anyone who attended the service of Holy Communion should receive the sacrament. In practice the weekly celebration desired by Church leaders was rare except in some private chapels or cathedrals. The problem was that congregations were reluctant to depart from the age-old custom of infrequent reception of the sacrament. This meant that parish celebrations of Holy Communion tended to be monthly at best and often only quarterly. Yet the standard format of the weekly Sunday liturgy was drawn in part from early sections of the rite of Holy Communion known as the Ante-Communion.

The insistence of the Church of England on a set liturgy was a significant factor in the eventual rejection of the ethos of the Established Church by many of the more radical Protestants. This took place during the Civil War and subsequently during the period of the Commonwealth. After the restoration of the monarchy and re-establishment of the Church of England in 1660 there were increasing moves for 'Non-Conformists' to separate completely from the Established Church. An insistence on typical Church of England liturgical structures and formulae is very strongly evident in the writings of George Herbert.

Herbert's country parson was more than simply a weaver of words. In the tradition of the Church of England, the priest's teaching role was expressed above all else in the leadership of liturgy or other forms of public prayer. Within the spirituality implicit in the *Book of Common Prayer* public worship, whether the Offices or the Holy Communion, was to be the main school of the Lord's service. The liturgy was the foundation of and the privileged expression of the 'common life' of the parish as a human and religious community. There is an almost Benedictine quality to this spirituality. For this reason, Herbert's parson was to give special attention to the dignity of public worship (Chapter VI 'The Parson Praying') and to the physical space, the church building and its furnishings, within which worship took place (Chapter XIII 'The Parson's Church'). This was an essential element of the pastoral care to be exercised by the priest.

George Herbert has an understandable bias towards a spirituality based on common prayer. In *The Country Parson* there are references to private prayer (for example, Chapter X 'The Parson in the House' and Chapter XXX 'The Parson in Liberty') and also to the guidance of individual people (Chapter XV 'The Parson Comforting' and Chapter XXXIV 'The Parson's Dexterity in Applying of Remedies'). However, his overall belief both in this work and in the poems is that common prayer is, as it were, prior to any exercises of private devotion and should be primary guide for the development of right belief, right attitudes and right action.

> Though private prayer be a brave design,
> Yet public hath more promises, more love:
> And love's a weight to hearts, to eyes a sign.
> We all are but cold suitors; let us move
> Where it is warmest. Leave thy six and seven;
> Pray with the most: for where most pray, is heaven.
>
> ('Perirrhanterium', ll. 396–402)

The Temple contains poems that celebrate the liturgical feasts such as 'Christmas', 'Lent', 'Good Friday', 'Easter', 'Whitsunday' and 'Trinity Sunday' and others that reflect liturgical or sacramental events such as 'Antiphon', 'Mattins', 'Evensong' or 'Holy Baptism'. Of course there are many explicit and implicit eucharistic references that I will discuss in the chapter on 'Prayer'. Other liturgical references are more indirect but none the less clear. For example, there is no poem entitled Advent but at least two poems evoke Advent themes. 'Grace' resonates with the Advent liturgy in its themes of longing and hope. The call of the poem that both grace and dew should 'Drop from above!' almost certainly refers directly to the words of the ancient Advent plainsong responsory, *Rorate caeli desuper et nubes pluant justum.* It is likely, in the context, that line 21, 'Oh come! for thou dost know the way', also echoes the Advent hymn *Veni, Veni, Emmanuel.* The poem 'Denial' also has an Advent flavour as it echoes the same hymn, '*Come, come, my God, O come*', and is immediately followed by the Christmas poems.

Scripture through Liturgy

Access by people to Scripture, and to biblical teaching, was central to the ethos of the Church of England. However, the English Reformation made liturgy and prayer the primary context for its reading and exposition. Thus, while an intellectual or theological approach to Scripture was present it was secondary. A theological reading of Scripture tends to address questions of belief or ethics. A liturgical or prayerful reading tends, rather, to seek resonances with human hopes and needs – not least the desire for intimacy with God.

When we turn to Herbert, can we actually separate the two great foundations of his spirituality, Scripture and the liturgy, or are they inseparable? Some commentators, reacting against what they perceive as an excessively 'Catholic' interpretation of Herbert, tend to reject liturgy as an independent context for his poems. For such writers, the Bible is the primary context for Herbert and is always a direct inspiration rather than mediated by references to the liturgy. However, at least two poems suggest that to distinguish sharply in this way between Scripture and the liturgy does damage to Herbert's special genius. 'Aaron' obviously uses a biblical reference to illustrate the distinction between an external holiness (symbolised by Aaron's dress) and the true holiness of head and heart symbolised by Christ. At the same time it is difficult to avoid the fairly clear references to the priest vesting for the liturgy. Interestingly, it is these liturgical references that seem to have caused a late seventeenth-century

Non-Conformist collection of hymns drawn from Herbert's poetry to censor certain parts of 'Aaron'!

'The Sacrifice' is the more famous example where a liturgical context for the biblical references is too explicit to be avoided. Here we can detect a particularly innovative fusion of Reformed and Catholic sensibilities. Nothing in Herbert is casual or accidental. Not only does 'The Sacrifice' follow the poem 'The Altar' but its cross and passion references underline a Reformation theology of the Eucharist. The Good Friday theme of 'The Sacrifice' does not refer directly to a Gospel narrative but to the liturgy of Holy Week. Interestingly, its use of the repetitive phrase 'Was ever grief like mine?' explicitly echoes the chanted *Improperia* of the pre-Reformation liturgy rather than the Prayer Book.

It seems that, at least in a few instances, the powerful significance of some of Herbert's biblical allusions would be diluted if their liturgical references were not also recognised. In the end, the Bible and the liturgy, the two great foundations of Herbert's spirituality – and indeed of the emerging Anglican spiritual tradition more generally – are too tightly interwoven to be artificially separated let alone ordered in some kind of clear priority. The peculiar genius of the British Church that Herbert celebrated depended on a creative tension between Reformed biblicism and Catholic liturgical sensibility.

3
The Image of God in Christ

> Christ is my only head,
> My alone only heart and breast,
> My only music, striking me ev'n dead;
> That to the old man I may rest,
> And be in him new drest.

> ('Aaron')

The reality of God is portrayed by George Herbert in terms of a strange mixture of majesty and intimacy. Indeed, it is the intimacy of God that stands out in Herbert as one of his strongest themes. The central focus of Herbert's poetry is the nature of God and the journey of the Christian person towards God. Because of this, Herbert's richest language about God appears more strikingly in the poetry than in *The Country Parson*.

If we begin with the poem 'Love III', which is the climax of the long central section of *The Temple*, two important aspects of Herbert's understanding of God stand out. First, God is a lover who woos the Christian soul rather than an impersonal power that seeks to impose an arbitrary and imperious will upon human beings. Second, the figure of Love in the poem is explicitly both creator ('Who made the eyes but I?') and redeemer ('who bore the blame?'). As we shall see later, Herbert is profoundly Christ-centred. What this implies is that, while Herbert's God is infinite and ultimately beyond our understanding, God's nature is also clearly revealed in and through the life and death of Jesus Christ. Arguably, too, the Holy Spirit is at least implicitly present in the poem. 'Love' is one of the Spirit's traditional designations and the Spirit's gift of sanctification, in which a person is made a 'guest . . .worthy to be here', clearly represents the overall dynamism of the poem.

The Freedom and Majesty of God

God appears throughout Herbert's writing as free and active. Indeed, the image of God as, predominantly, the active partner in the divine-human relationship runs throughout both the prose treatise and the poems. In some respects, *The Country Parson* presents a more awesome picture of God than the poems. The parson is 'truly touched and amazed with the Majesty of God' (Chapter VI). He is to adore humbly the invisible majesty of God every time he enters the church building (Chapter VIII). This is the approach to God that the priest is also to encourage in the congregation. The priest is continually to preach the presence and majesty of God. God is very holy, great and terrible. Yet, if God is great in judgement, God is also great in mercy (Chapter VII).

In numerous places in Herbert's portrayal of God there is a tension between otherness and intimacy. His 'Prayer Before Sermon' at the end of *The Country Parson* begins with a strong emphasis on the otherness of God. 'Oh Almighty and everliving Lord God! Majesty, and Power, and Brightness, and Glory! How shall we dare to appear before thy face, who are contrary to thee, in all we call thee?' Yet the prayer moves forward to acknowledge that God exalts mercy above everything else and so 'thou, Lord, art patience and pity, and sweetness, and love'. God is all-powerful. However, this power does not merely govern the created order but sustains and preserves it and turns all things to blessing and advantage (Chapter XXX). In prayer we may say to God,

> Oh what supreme almighty power
> Is thy great arm which spans the east and west,
> And tacks the centre to the sphere!

Yet we must also say,

> Of what immeasurable love
> Art thou possest . . .
> > ('Prayer II')

At several points in the poems, Herbert is prepared to acknowledge the wrath of God (for example in the poems 'Sighs and Groans', 'Complaining', 'Bitter-Sweet'). The wrath of God relates to sin but as the poem 'Faith' makes clear, while

> . . . sin placeth me in Adam's fall,
> Faith sets me higher in his glory.

When justified by faith in Jesus Christ, we flawed humans may look forward to the fulfilment of our vocation as creatures which is union with God.

The Loving Intimacy of God

Interestingly, God's freedom and action is most powerfully expressed not as detachment and judgement but as love. 'My God, thou art all love' ('Evensong'). In 'Love I' God is 'Immortal Love' and in 'Love II' is addressed as 'Immortal Heat' whose 'flame' kindles in us true desires.

> It is thy highest art
> To captivate strong holds to thee.
>
> ('Nature')

For Herbert, God's action is always at the heart of things. Even so, human beings are not purely passive in their relationship with God. As we have already seen, the seventeenth century saw an increasing tension in Anglican circles between an emphasis on the sovereignty of God's will and human freedom and co-operation with God's action. For George Herbert, although God's action is always at the heart of things, our human response to God is equally important. Human beings are creatures of desire who (as Herbert himself appears to do in his poetry) struggle to reach out to God in response. God is the one 'who giveth me my Desires and Performances' (Preface to *The Country Parson*).

> For my heart's desire
> Unto thine is bent:
> I aspire
> To a full consent.
>
> ('Discipline')

Herbert understands that God woos the human soul sensitively rather than forces or overpowers it. 'Thou didst entice to thee my heart' ('Affliction I'). This enables Herbert to allow for a certain reciprocity between God and human creatures.

> My God, what is a heart,
> That thou shouldst it so eye, and woo,
> Pouring upon it all thy art,
> As if that thou hadst nothing else to do?
>
> ('Mattins')

It is interesting to compare the poetry of George Herbert with that of the nineteenth-century Jesuit Gerard Manley Hopkins. It appears that Herbert's image of God is to some degree the opposite of Hopkins'. For Herbert, as opposed to Hopkins, God is not terrible, overwhelming or dominating – the awesome transcendent Other. Interestingly, Hopkins is never able to be angry or 'peevish' with God in the way Herbert feels free to be. Although in Herbert's works, God is utterly holy ('I cannot look on thee' in 'Love III'), his conflicts are within the context of an intimate relationship. His fundamental assurance and starting point is always God's love rather than God's judgement or wrath. God is a gracious and tolerant Father (Chapter XXXI 'The Parson in Liberty'). The poem 'Sacrifice' vividly portrays the fickleness and sinfulness of humanity even in the face of the cross but, as in the First Week of the Ignatian *Spiritual Exercises*, God's sole response is one of generosity rather than judgement. Even the poem 'Discipline' which speaks of God's wrath, invites God to

> Throw away thy rod,
> Throw away thy wrath.

Indeed in the final stanza of the poem Herbert seems to suggest that, because God is God, wrath is unnecessary, even inappropriate 'Though man frailties hath'. God's love is actually more powerful and effective than anger.

> Love will do the deed:
> For with love
> Stony hearts will bleed.

Herbert's sense of God's presence and intimacy is thoroughly 'incarnational'. God is not removed from human life or the created world but is to be found, and responded to, in the ordinary and the everyday. Indeed, for Herbert, it is everyday events and tasks rather than the glories of nature that catch his attention most of all. God is present with the priest even as he enters the poorest cottage 'For both God is there also, and those for whom God died' (Chapter XIV). In the poem 'Redemption', God in Christ is to be found in the midst of

> . . . a ragged noise and mirth
> Of thieves and murderers . . .

Herbert finds God in the everyday round, as for example in 'The Elixir', the words of which became a well-loved hymn.

> Teach me, my God and King,
> In all things thee to see,
> And what I do in any thing,
> To do it as for thee:

Nothing is outside the loving providence of God. No aspect of human life is beneath contempt. Nothing is too small for God. 'Thou art in small things great, not small in any' ('Providence'). Herbert's spirituality of everyday life will be examined more broadly in the next chapter.

Apart from everyday actions and events, George Herbert experiences the presence and action of God most strongly within himself and in the celebration of the Eucharist. One of the most important images of *The Temple* is God dwelling and working within the human heart (for example, the poems entitled 'The Altar' and 'The Church Floor'). The sacramental theme is so pervasive that it would be tedious to list all the poems where the Eucharist is mentioned or implied. Herbert's eucharistic spirituality will be developed further in the chapter on prayer. Indeed, intimacy with God is often expressed sacramentally in Herbert. In 'The Agony' the association between the experience of God as Love, the cross and reception of Communion is tightly drawn. The poem makes a particularly deft connection between blood and wine that powerfully relates together God's intimacy to us, redemption and sacramental theology.

> Who knows not Love, let him assay
> And taste that juice, which on the cross a pike
> Did set again abroach; then let him say
> If ever he did taste the like.
> Love is that liquor sweet and most divine,
> Which my God feels as blood; but I, as wine.
>
> (ll. 13–18)

The particular intimacy between God and those who preside at the Eucharist, and the burden this lays upon them, is mentioned in *The Country Parson* (Chapter XXII) and in the poem 'The Priesthood'.

> But th' holy men of God such vessels are,
> As serve him up, who all the world commands:
> When God vouchsafeth to become our fare,

Their hands convey him, who conveys their hands.
Oh what pure things, most pure must those things be,
Who bring my God to me!

(ll. 25–30)

Perhaps the single poem that most graphically illustrates Herbert's sense of the intimacy of God is the one entitled 'Clasping of Hands'. Human desire is for a union between us and God that somehow transcends 'Thine' and 'Mine'.

Lord, thou art mine, and I am thine,
If mine I am: and thine much more,
Than I or ought, or can be mine.
Yet to be thine, doth me restore;
So that again I now am mine,
And with advantage mine the more.
Since this being mine, brings with it thine,
And thou with me dost thee restore.
If I without thee would be mine,
I neither should be mine nor thine.

Lord, I am thine, and thou art mine:
So mine thou art, that something more
I may presume thee mine, than thine.
For thou didst suffer to restore
Not thee, but me, and to be mine,
And with advantage mine the more.
Since thou in death wast none of thine,
Yet then as mine didst me restore.
Oh be mine still! Still make me thine!
Or rather make no Thine and Mine!

The Trinity

If Herbert's God is a strange mixture of distant majesty and intimacy, how does he employ the classical Christian image of God, the Trinity? There are not many direct allusions to the Trinity in *The Temple*. There is a possible musical image in the 'three parts' of the final stanza of 'Easter'. There is a clear reference in the poem 'Trinity Sunday'. The first stanza suggests the classic threefold titles of creator, redeemer and sanctifier.

> Lord, thou has form'd me out of mud,
> And hast redeem'd me through thy blood,
> And sanctifi'd me to do good;

There also seem to be three triads in the final stanza that, as it were, express the desired impact or reflection of the Trinity in Herbert's life.

> Enrich my heart, mouth, hands in me,
> With faith, with hope, with charity;
> That I may run, rise, rest with thee.

Herbert's relative reticence about God as Trinity is perhaps explained in the poem 'Ungratefulness'. Here Herbert suggests that God

> . . . hast but two rare cabinets full of treasure
> The *Trinity* and *Incarnation*.

He continues:

> The statelier cabinet is the *Trinity*,
> Whose sparkling light access denies:

> Therefore thou dost not show
> This fully to us, till death blow
> The dust into our eyes:
> For by that powder thou wilt make us see.

However, it is the incarnation that can 'allure us' at this point. This is the more immediate and attractive treasure.

Certainly it is difficult to discover evidence of sharp distinctions between the traditional attributes of the persons of the Trinity. Herbert regularly changes focus from God as creator to God as redeemer. The Lord of the poem 'Longing' is 'Lord JESU' (line 73) and the one who

> . . . didst bow
> Thy dying head upon the tree.
>
> (ll. 31–2)

Yet the Lord is also, implicitly, the God who has created ('Indeed the world's thy book', line 49) and whose 'duty' is to continue to sustain:

> To thee help appertains.
> Hast thou left all things to their course,
> And laid the reins
> Upon the horse?
>
> (ll. 42–6)

Once again, in the poem 'Redemption' it is the rich Lord of heaven who goes to earth as Son. One of the central poems of the collection, 'The Sacrifice', uses the structure of the Reproaches from the traditional Catholic liturgy for Good Friday to express the grief of Christ on the cross. Yet the figure who grieves on the cross is also the maker (line 6), 'he that built the world' (line

67), the one who gives breath (line 70), the Lord of hosts (line 79) and the one who lives eternally (line 99).

A Christ-centred Spirituality

In 'The Church', the central portion of *The Temple* (and the 'temple' is, partly, Christ), nearly all Herbert's poems concern Christ or are directly addressed to him. Christ is at the centre of the Christian's life, carved in the human heart.

> JESU is in my heart, his sacred name
> Is deeply carved there: but th'other week
> A great affliction broke the little frame,
> Ev'n all to pieces: which I went to seek:
> And first I found the corner, where was *J*,
> After, where *ES*, and next where *U* was graved.
> When I had got these parcels, instantly
> I sat me down to spell them, and perceived
> That to my broken heart he was *I ease you*,
> And to my whole is *JESU*.
>
> ('JESU')

Yet Herbert's Christology is not greatly concerned with the life of the human Jesus compared to Catholic Reformation spirituality such as that of Ignatius Loyola. This is true even when Herbert suggests that the Christian life should reflect the double state of the life of 'our Saviour'. 'These two states were in our Saviour, not only in the beginning of his preaching, but afterwards also, as *Matthew* 22:35. He was tempted: And *Luke* 10:21. He rejoiced in the Spirit' (*The Country Parson*, Chapter XXXIV). Herbert's emphasis is always strongly on the cross. In 'The Bag' Christ's wounded side becomes as it were the safe deposit for our messages to God. Our way to holiness is not Christ-focused devotion or 'imitation of Christ' in mission but to accept God's grace revealed in Christ, especially in the passion, and to trust in it. Throughout all our struggles and uncertainties, our ultimate assurance is the triumph of Christ expressed in the poem 'Easter':

> Who takes thee by the hand, that thou likewise
> With him mayst rise.

As we have seen, Herbert tends to blend together the eternal creator God and the suffering Christ on the cross. So, at Holy Communion we 'receive God' (*The Country Parson*, Chapter XXII). In the poem 'Easter Wings' the 'Lord, who createdst man in wealth and store' and the Saviour are one and the same. This blending tends to outweigh any sense of a harsh version of the 'penal substitution' theory of the passion. God is revealed as love rather than as a judge and this love is known especially in Christ. The lesson of 'The Sacrifice' is that we cannot finally defeat God's love. Even our refusals of love merely serve to reveal further depths of love in God's patient endurance. Herbert's frequent use of the title 'Lord' for God is not, therefore, a matter of power. Indeed, God seems closest when met precisely as the Lord who is courteous or who, for example in 'Redemption', does a favour or 'grants a suit'. There is even a modest hint of a feminine image for God in the poem 'Longing' where, as in Julian of Norwich, human motherhood is a reflection of God.

> From thee all pity flows.
> Mothers are kind, because thou art,
> And dost dispose

To them a part:
Their infants, them; and they suck thee
More free.

The Absence of God

In tension with this strong sense of presence and God's loving intimacy in Christ, is a sense of God's absence or hiddenness. This common spiritual experience appears in a number of Herbert's poems. 'The Search' expresses how profoundly painful this is.

Whither, Oh, whither art thou fled,
My Lord, my Love?
My searches are my daily bread;
Yet never prove.

Faithfulness and discipline in prayer cannot, on their own, assuage the sense of bemusement at God's apparent absence but rather deepen it.

My knees pierce th' earth, mine eyes the sky;
And yet the sphere
And centre both to me deny
That thou are there.

Sometimes, as the poem 'Denial' suggests, it is easier to give up the struggle when God does not seem to hear and there is no feeling apart from a vague discontent.

Oh cheer and tune my heartless breast,
Defer no time;

That so thy favours granting my request,
They and my mind may chime,
And mend my rhyme.

Somehow a deepening of faith is implied. As 'The Search' hints, we struggle to touch God and yet much of the time we are called to walk by faith alone and not by sight or sense. Another poem 'Longing' suggests that God sometimes deliberately withholds consolation for reasons that are impossible to fathom. Ultimately, God's way of seeing and acting is inscrutable. Perhaps Herbert's mode of expressing the experience hints at specifically Protestant sensibilities – the *deus absconditus* of Luther and the sovereign will of God of Calvin. However, the experience that Herbert describes is the common currency of all Christians who struggle with God. The Christian tradition has always balanced a sense of God's intimacy and revelation in creation and in Christ with a sense of our inability to possess God or to fathom God's ultimate mystery.

4

'In All Things Thee to See':
Incarnational Spirituality

We have already seen that George Herbert, like so many early representatives of the Anglican spiritual tradition, had a strong sense of God's presence in the world and of God's involvement with the human condition. For this reason, seventeenth-century Anglican spirituality has often been described as particularly 'incarnational'. Its central emphasis is that God is committed to the world as creator and this commitment is further underlined in God's action of redeeming the world in Christ. The God of Christianity is thoroughly engaged with time and space rather than detached from them. These perspectives affirm something vital about God. But the notion of an incarnate God also says something very important about the value of the material world and of everyday human life. The whole of human existence, our minds and bodies as well as our spirit dimension, are gifts of God. The world is the theatre of God's activity and a place of soul making rather than simply an unhappy vale of tears. Nothing is unimportant to God and, for us humans, everything has the capacity to unlock eternity.

> Thou art in small things great, not small in any:
> Thy even praise can neither rise, nor fall.

Thou art in all things one, in each thing many:
For thou art infinite in one and all.

                              ('Providence')

As we shall see, Herbert does give some attention to the natural world as a second book of revelation alongside the Scriptures. However, compared to other well-known seventeenth-century Anglican writers such as Thomas Traherne or Henry Vaughan, Herbert's attention is focused less on the sacred quality of nature or landscape and rather more on finding God in everyday *events* and in human *action*. As we shall see in the next chapter, even Herbert's sense of place is closely associated with the life and activities of specific communities of people.

A Spirituality of Time

A concern to seek and find God in the everyday necessarily involves viewing 'time' as important. Because Herbert's spirituality is so liturgical it is hardly surprising that for him 'time' is imbued with spiritual significance. Although his poem 'Time' indicates an ambivalent attitude on his part, it certainly suggests that, because of Christ's coming, time is no longer the destroyer of human aspirations. 'Time' has become the gardener who prunes us so that we might grow properly and moves us towards union with God.

And in his [Christ's] blessing thou art blest
For where thou only wert before
An executioner at best;
Thou art a gard'ner now, and more,

44

An usher to convey our souls
Beyond the utmost stars and poles.

It has sometimes been suggested that the doctrine of Christ's resurrection destroys time. However, a Christian view of time cannot view it as ultimately valueless. Christ's resurrection overcomes time only as *a symbol of the destruction of human hopes and meaning*. Time itself is not so much destroyed as transfigured and given a wholly new significance. Herbert hints at this when he suggests that time is now the channel that draws us inexorably towards a destiny that is full of promise.

The liturgical sensibilities of Anglicanism that Herbert so deeply shared has always given significant attention to the importance of time in the shaping of spirituality. Of course this is also thoroughly biblical because the origins of liturgy lie in the Jewish roots of Christianity and, as Abraham Heschel suggested so beautifully in his book *The Sabbath*, Judaism is a religion of time. Time is the architecture of holiness because it is there that human beings can discover the reality of eternity with which time is imbued. At the most basic level, the spiritual significance of time is underlined and shaped in the celebration of liturgical seasons and festivals, in the daily rhythm of common prayer, in the cycle of Scripture readings and in the monthly cycle for the recitation of the psalms. In a general sense, the liturgical attention to 'time' is intended to connect our relationship with time to the overall process of our daily lives.

However, there is a deeper level to the spirituality of time that Herbert was able to enter through the liturgy as much as through the Bible. Liturgy, and especially the Eucharist, brings our particular moment of time into living contact with all time, past, present and future. Time and eternity intersect in this 'thin' moment. It becomes 'heaven in ordinary', 'the six-days-world transposing in an hour'. Thus, in his poem 'Sunday', Herbert suggests that this particular weekly time, associated with public liturgy, is a kind of doorway from ordinary 'time' to eternity.

> The Sundays of man's life,
> Threaded together on time's string,
> Make bracelets to adorn the wife
> Of the eternal glorious King.
> On Sunday heaven's gate stands ope;
> Blessings are plentiful and rife,
> More plentiful than hope.

Of course the ultimate doorway to eternity is what Herbert's Celtic spiritual ancestors forever sought in their ascetical wanderings, the 'place of resurrection'. This was a location in the physical landscape, chosen by God and particular to each, where a person was to settle to await death, that ultimate doorway into eternal life. But a special 'place' also implies a special 'time' – the time of our death. So, Herbert suggests, the year of our lives that is most fruitful is the one which brings the ultimate harvesting 'when we leave our corn and hay' and also encounter 'The last and lov'd, though dreadful day' ('Home').

The Created World

Without doubt Herbert appreciated the natural world as a context for experiencing the presence and activity of God. He does not simply describe the beauty of nature from time to time but employs natural images in other ways. In an interesting link between time and the natural world, Sunday, according to his poem of the same name, is 'the next world's bud'. The other days of the week 'are the fruitful beds and borders of God's rich garden'. And 'God's rich garden' is the garden of the world. The month of May 'straw'd with flowers and happiness' becomes a striking image of Herbert's fresh and youthful faith before he entered into a deeper spiritual struggle ('Affliction I'). And, once again, when God returns to us, as it were, after periods of spiritual darkness, snow melting in May and the flowering of springtime provide the evocative images ('The Flower'). The orange tree, laden with fruit ('that busy plant!'), becomes an image of Herbert's desire to bear spiritual fruit for God the gardener ('Employment II').

Herbert has a particular fondness for the imagery of bees and herbs. Bees represent productive lives not least when Herbert expresses his deep desire to serve God usefully ('Employment I') or when he laments his spiritual weakness ('Praise I'). Bees also become an image of the natural wisdom that all creatures have that enables God's providence to express itself effectively in the world's workings.

> Bees work for man; and yet they never bruise
> Their master's flower, but leave it, having done,
> As fair as ever, and as fit to use;
> So both the flower doth stay, and honey run.
>
> ('Providence')

Heaven may be compared to a hive to which our lives are drawn like laden bees.

> Surely thou wilt joy, by gaining me
> To fly home like a laden bee

47

Unto that hive of beams
And garland-streams.
　　　　　('The Star')

George Herbert in *The Country Parson* recommends that the
parish priest and his family should ideally be expert in herbs and
herbal medicine (Chapter XXIII). Herbert employs his herbal
expertise to great effect in the poetry. Like herbs, the Scriptures
are a kind of balm or cure for our human ills. Just as 'dispersed
herbs' may be brought together to create a powerful medicine,
so diverse parts of Scripture may illuminate each other to 'make
up some Christian's destiny' ('The Holy Scriptures II').

For all that Herbert relishes natural imagery and offers a
positive view of the created order, his vision is not merely
romantic or a form of nature mysticism. Creation is the second
book of revelation precisely because it draws us to the deeper
truth of God's reality, loving presence and powerful action.

Indeed the world's thy book,
Where all things have their leaf assign'd:
Yet a meek look
Hath interlin'd.
Thy board is full, yet humble guests
Find nests.
　　　　　　('Longing')

For Herbert this ability to discern the reality of God in all things
is uniquely human.

The bird that sees a dainty bower
Made in the tree, where she was wont to sit,
Wonders and sings, but not his power
Who made the arbour: this exceeds her wit.

48

But Man doth know
The spring, whence all things flow:
(‘Misery’)

The poem ‘Misery’ not only expresses Herbert’s deep sense of nature as a revelation of God but also the danger of overlooking the presence of the creator within the created order and of confining our wonder to what is partial rather than extending it to what is All. Herbert’s mystical sense is always focused beyond the immediate, beyond the appearance of things, to the ultimate source of beauty and goodness. There are undoubtedly echoes here of the Wisdom literature of the Hebrew Scriptures of which Herbert was particularly fond if not an explicit allusion to the Wisdom of Solomon.

For all people who were ignorant of God were foolish by
nature;
and they were unable from the good things that are seen
to know the one who exists,
nor did they recognise the artisan while paying heed to his
works;
but they supposed that either fire or wind or swift air,
or the circle of the stars, or turbulent water,
or the luminaries of heaven were the gods that rule the
world.
If through delight in the beauty of these things people
assumed them to be gods,
let them know how much better than these is their Lord,
for the author of beauty created them.
And if people were amazed at their power and working,
let them perceive from them
how much more powerful is the one who formed them.

For from the greatness and beauty of created things
comes a corresponding perception of their Creator.
Yet these people are little to be blamed,
for perhaps they go astray
while seeking God and desiring to find him.
For while they live among his works, they keep searching,
and they trust in what they see, because the things that are
    seen are beautiful.
Yet again, not even they are to be excused;
for if they had the power to know so much
that they could investigate the world,
how did they fail to find sooner the Lord of these things?

                (The Wisdom of Solomon 13:1–9)

The Everyday

Herbert belongs to a broad tradition of spirituality that places most emphasis on seeking and finding God in the ordinary and everyday. It is tempting to seek direct connections between George Herbert and those Roman Catholic spiritualities that were known in England in his day. For example, those associated with Ignatius Loyola or Francis de Sales had a similar emphasis on finding God in everyday life. It is likely that Herbert, like his friend Nicholas Ferrar, was aware of de Sales. However, Herbert's preoccupation with the everyday is just as likely to be rooted partly in his strong liturgical sense and partly in Reformation sensitivities. The latter tended to emphasise first of all engage-ment with God in the ordinary rather than in mystical illuminations, then a certain equality of experience among

Christians that tended to favour everyday contexts and finally a strong sense that our relationship with God would be expressed in moral action. Thus the long poem 'Perirrhanterium' that forms the bulk of the first section of *The Temple* is often seen as relatively uninspiring and moral in tone. Yet it also establishes a firm foundation for the more personal struggles in the later poems by focusing our attention on the events of daily life and on concern for other people.

Probably the best-known example of a spirituality of the everyday is the words of the hymn 'Teach me, my God and King'.

Teach me, my God and King,
In all things thee to see,
And what I do in any thing,
To do it as for thee:

Not rudely, as a beast,
To run into an action;
But still to make thee prepossest,
And give it his perfection.

A man that looks on glass,
On it may stay his eye;
Or if he pleaseth, through it pass,
And then the heav'n espy.

All may of thee partake:
Nothing can be so mean,
Which with his tincture (for thy sake)
Will not grow bright and clean.

> A servant with this clause
> Make drudgery divine:
> Who sweeps a room, as for thy laws,
> Makes that and th' action fine.
>
> This is the famous stone
> That turneth all to gold:
> For that which God doth touch and own
> Cannot for less be told.
>
> ('The Elixir')

On the one hand, the magic formula, the alchemist's stone, is simply to do everything, however small, as an act of praise of God. There are parallels here to the great Carmelite mystics Teresa of Avila and Brother Lawrence and their spirituality of finding God amongst the pots and pans or to Thérèse of Lisieux and her 'little way'. Nothing is too ordinary and nothing too small to be the focus for our contemplative vision. However, the sense of the final stanza is richer still. God does not 'touch' the ordinary in a simple sense. 'To touch' in reference to fine metals such as gold refers to the touchstone used to test the purity of the metal. Equally, once 'touched' (that is, tested), the metals were marked with their standard of purity. So, our 'ordinary' lives lived out for God are tested and accepted by God and declared to be pure gold.

Beauty, Music and Poetry

George Herbert was someone with deep aesthetic sensibilities. We have already seen how he appreciated the beauties of liturgy and of church buildings and their power to make an impact on the human spirit. Apart from the imaginative qualities of his own poetry, we know that Herbert had a deep love of music and was an able musician in his own right. He had a particular appreciation of Church music which he suggested was 'the way to heaven's door' ('Church-music'). There is a telling paragraph in Isaak Walton's *The Life of Mr George Herbert* (pp. 371–2).

> His chiefest recreation was music, in which heavenly art he was a most excellent master, and did himself compose many divine hymns and anthems, which he set and sung to his lute or viol; and though he was a lover of retiredness, yet his love to music was such, that he went usually twice every week on certain appointed days to the cathedral church in Salisbury; and at his return would say, that his time spent in prayer and cathedral music elevated his soul, and was his heaven upon earth. But before his return thence to Bemerton, he would usually sing and play his part at an appointed private music meeting; and, to justify this practice, he would often say, religion does not banish mirth, but only moderates and sets rules to it.

Clearly Herbert felt the need to justify his love and practice of music against the more stringent Puritan party within the Church. His prose text *The Country Parson* offers few examples of this sensitivity. It is essentially a didactic and moralistic text and its austere tone hardly expresses Herbert's own creative abilities. We have to turn to Herbert's poems for any real indication of this side of his temperament and spirituality. In *The Temple* musical images abound and it is possible to make only a small selection to give a flavour of Herbert's vision.

Musical imagery (and possibly a reference to his actual music-making) is used to express Herbert's intense desire to respond to Christ's grief and passion ('The Sacrifice').

> My music shall find thee, and ev'ry string
> Shall have his attribute to sing;
> That all together may accord in thee,
> And prove one God, one harmony.
>
> ('The Thanksgiving')

Herbert found that musical images had a particular power to express praise of God. In the poem 'Praise II', which has become a popular hymn, Herbert promises,

> Wherefore with my utmost art
> I will sing thee.

In the poem 'Easter', Herbert greets the risen Easter Lord with the image of lute playing. Christ's arms stretched on the cross are compared to the taut strings of the lute that are tuned to just the right pitch to make the appropriate notes. Herbert calls on God's Spirit to 'bear a part' and thus enrich the imperfect harmony of human attempts to praise God.

> Awake, my lute, and struggle for thy part
> With all thy art.
> The cross taught all wood to resound his name,
> Who bore the same.
> His stretched sinews taught all strings, what key
> Is best to celebrate this most high day.
>
> Consort both heart and lute, and twist a song
> Pleasant and long:
> Or since all music is but three parts vied

> And multiplied,
> O let thy blessed Spirit bear a part,
> And make up our defects with his sweet art.
>
> ('Easter')

The image of tuning is also used to express the ways that God seeks to enable the growth of human sinners.

> Yet take thy way; for sure thy way is best:
> Stretch or contract me, thy poor debtor:
> This is but tuning of my breast,
> To make the music better.
>
> ('The Temper I')

Equally, Herbert uses the image of tuning for moments when he suffered from spiritual dryness. His soul was 'untun'd, unstrung' and he begs God to 'mend my rhyme' and to 'cheer and tune my heartless breast' ('Denial').

Herbert thought of poetry as itself a form of prayer. Interestingly, lyric poetry underwent a particularly important moment of development at the time that Herbert was writing. Lyric verse had particular associations with love poetry and also with movement or change. Both of these associations were taken and used by Herbert as a means of portraying the seasons of the soul and the intensity of his love relationship with God.

At times, poetry seems scarcely adequate to praise God.

> To write a verse or two, is all the praise,
> That I can raise.
>
> ('Praise I')

For all its limitations, however, Herbert is able to declare that poetry is a means of communion with God.

But it is that which while I use
I am with thee . . .
                ('The Quiddity')

Behind Herbert's aesthetic appreciation lies a sense of the beauty of God. Herbert's appreciation of created beauty is expressed less in terms of aesthetics pure and simple and more in terms of the ways creation reflects the beauty of God. It is humankind's particular gift to be able to discern the presence of God in all things. To praise the beauty and value of human activities such as making music or writing poetry was also to praise God. On the other hand, the beauty of human phrases or compositions is merely a pale reflection of God's beauty. 'Immortal love' is 'that beauty which can never fade' ('Love I'). And

True beauty dwells on high: ours is a flame
But borrow'd thence to light us thither.

                        ('The Forerunners')

Thus, for all that Herbert loved music so deeply, in the end he would affirm that

Christ is my only head,
My alone only heart and breast,
My only music . . .

        ('Aaron')

5

A Sense of Place

A sense of place or locality is central to Herbert's spiritual vision. It is an important key to his description of the localised ministry of the country parson. An emphasis on the church building as sacred place also acts as one of the frameworks for *The Temple*.

There is an intimate connection between our sense of place and a realisation of God 'placed' in the heart of human life. Anglican spirituality seems to have a particularly strong sense of place. Some commentators have pointed to close connections between the understanding of liturgy and of the worshipping community in the *Book of Common Prayer* and the unusual degree of influence by Benedictine monasticism on the origins and subsequent history of the English Church. So perhaps 'place' in Herbert has something to do with a residual, if unconscious, echo of the monastic virtue of stability. However, there are probably more immediate reasons. The simplest one is that the Church of England was heir to the pre-Reformation pattern of geographical parishes. It continued to stand for a 'community' model of Church rather than for the gathered or associational model that inevitably came to be the norm for dissenters, whether Puritans or Roman Catholics. Again, the Church of England model of priesthood was not something that existed in its own right in splendid theological isolation but was grounded, or 'located', in relationship to a specific community where the Word of God was preached and the sacraments celebrated. In a more general way, Anglican identity from the very beginning was not based on tightly defined core doctrines or innovative and distinctive structures but rather on a shared history and a sense of continuities and present connections. In other words, Anglicanism has a great deal to do with community life, which means people and places – indeed, people *in* places.

A sense of place, its relationship to individual and collective memory, and its impact on human identity, have become major preoccupations in contemporary Western culture. This is a spiritual issue of great importance. One of its central features is the search for 'home'. A vision of home, family and household is an important theme in Herbert's *The Country Parson*.

The Household

According to Herbert, the priest's household, like the monastery of *The Rule of St Benedict* (Prologue 45), is a 'school of the Lord's service'. It is a place of spiritual nurture, education, ministry and hospitality as well as a context for establishing a proper rhythm for living. There are striking parallels with the Christian humanist Sir Thomas More who placed an equally strong emphasis on the spirituality of home and family. More's organisation of his household as a spiritual reality some hundred years before Herbert follows similar patterns. In both cases parents, children, servants and guests share in a balanced and rhythmic life of prayer, study, sober recreation and service of neighbour. It has been said that More organised his household as a form of lay monastery. In his case, there was a personal affinity with the austere Carthusian Order with which More had had close associations in his youth. Herbert lived in a very different religious world but one cannot help wondering whether the form of lay monasticism practised by his great friend Nicholas Ferrar and his family at Little Gidding had some influence. It is just possible that both men shared an awareness of the teaching on the 'mixed life' (contemplation and action) written for reforming clergy and devout lay people by the fourteenth-century spiritual teacher Walter Hilton. His works were certainly highly influential in reforming circles in More's time and there is some thought that they may have continued to circulate in England after the Reformation and have been accessible to seventeenth-century Anglicans.

Herbert's description of the home and household of the priest also has a quasi-monastic quality. Yet its purpose is not to be seen in isolation. It is to be 'a copy and model for his parish' (Chapter X). The priest studies, prays and works within the framework of a community life both within the household and within the wider parish. The priest is to be someone of learning. Although the most vital 'learning' is spiritual rather than intellectual, it is clear from all the references in *The Country Parson* that the house is, like a good Benedictine monastery, to have a well-stocked library. Just as Thomas More encouraged the education of other members of his household, including the women, so Herbert expects all the members of the priest's home to share to some degree in the ministry. So 'home' is a place where the Christian life is lived with some intensity and, as the poem 'The Family' makes clear, home is also where God dwells.

> But, Lord, the house and family are thine,
> Though some of them repine.

Turn out these wranglers, which defile thy seat:
For where thou dwellest all is neat.

The Church

Another significant element of Herbert's sense of place was the church building. He had a very positive understanding of God's presence in the church. The use of the words 'Temple' and 'Church' in his great poetic collection works on several levels. The community of the Church is the Body of Christ and the individual soul is the temple of the Holy Spirit. But alongside these the building itself is seen as a sacred place. The parish church is, like the Jewish Temple, a place of meeting between humans and God. Herbert describes the parish priest on entering the church 'humbly adoring, and worshipping the invisible majesty and presence of Almighty God' (*The Country Parson*, Chapter VIII). Baptism takes place there 'in the presence of God and his saints' (Chapter XXII). In the poem 'Perirrhanterium' Herbert exhorts the reader to show special respect in church buildings for it is God's house not just a human meeting place.

God is more there, than thou: for thou art there
Only by his permission . . .

(11. 404–5)

Elsewhere he suggests that a 'godly' person may well have a custom of dropping into church for a brief prayer. This is not superstition but 'reverence to God's house' and an occasion to thank God for dwelling in our midst (Chapter XXXI).

The building and its furnishings all have significance and point us towards a life of holiness. Herbert's poems *The Temple* are structured to suggest a journey from the outer 'Church Porch' (the first section, full of moral exhortation and preparation) into the 'Church' itself (the central section which includes the poems of greatest spiritual depth). In Herbert's way of seeing things, the actual arrangement of the church speaks not only of liturgical functions but also of a spirituality of journey and pilgrimage. Throughout the poems there is a scattering of brief references to the physical features of the building acting as a medium for spiritual encounters. So for example in 'The Elixir',

> A man that looks on glass,
> On it may stay his eye;
> Or if he pleaseth, through it pass,
> And then the heav'n espy.

There are also poems dedicated to parts of the building. There is only time here to hint at a few examples of their spiritual message. The very first poem of the central section is 'The Altar'. This stands not only for the theological centrality of Christ's cross and passion but also for the central action of the community within the building, the Eucharist, that makes effective in the present the saving actions of Christ. However, Herbert's reflections suggest that the altar that really matters is the human heart.

> A broken ALTAR, Lord, thy servant rears,
> Made of a heart, and cemented with tears.

'Church Monuments' uses the tombs and memorials in the building as a focus for meditation on the frailty of human life.

Dear flesh, while I do pray, learn here thy stem
And true descent; that when thou shalt grow fat,
And wanton in thy cravings, thou mayst know,
That flesh is but the glass, which holds the dust
That measures all our time; which also shall
Be crumpled into dust.

'The Church Lock and Key' reminds the reader that what shuts us out from God's presence is only our sinfulness and the lack of desire.

I know it is my sin, which locks thine ears,
            And binds thy hands;
Out-crying my requests, drowning my tears;
Or else the chillness of my faint demands.

The solidity of the stones and steps of 'The Church Floor' speak to Herbert of the qualities of patience, humility, confidence, love and charity. These virtues are the solid stones of human holiness but only because the divine architect builds 'so strong in a weak heart'.

Mark you the floor? That square and speckled stone,
        Which looks so firm and strong,
            Is *Patience:*

And th' other black and grave, wherewith each one
        Is checker'd all along,
            Humility:

The gentle rising, which on either hand
        Leads to the Choir above,
            Is *Confidence:*

> But the sweet cement, which in one sure band
> Ties the whole frame, is *Love*
> And *Charity*.

Finally, in 'The Windows' Herbert implies that the colours and light of the windows themselves in 'this glorious and transcendent place' have the power to reveal God's story. Yet just as the colours are fixed in the glass when it is fired so God's life is, as it were, fixed and fired into the holy preacher and shines forth. Without this, a preacher's many words in the building are empty things that on their own 'Doth vanish like a flaring thing'.

In a sense the particular visible expression of the Body of Christ to which Herbert gave his loyalty, the national Church, was also a 'sacred' place. It was local and particular yet also part of the universal Church Catholic. These sentiments are clearly expressed in Herbert's poem 'The British Church'. 'She on the hills' (Rome) 'wantonly allureth all' with her 'painted shrines'. 'She in the valley' (Geneva), on the contrary was

> . . . so shy
> Of dressing, that her hair doth lie
> About her ears.

The Church of England is for Herbert his 'dearest Mother'. Her way is the middle way: 'The mean thy praise and glory is'.

Herbert's loyalty to the Church was expressed practically in his attitude to his bishop as spiritual father and to the diocese as the local Church. Herbert's vision of a priest was by no means freewheeling or autonomous.

> He carries himself very respectfully, as to all the Fathers of the Church, so especially to his Diocesan, honouring him both in word and behaviour, and resorting unto him in any

difficulty, either in his studies or in his parish. He observes Visitations, and being there, makes due use of them, as of clergy councils, for the benefit of the diocese. And therefore before he comes, having observed some defects in the ministry, he then either in sermon, if he preach, or at some other time of the day, propounds among his brethren what were fitting to be done. (*The Country Parson*, Chapter XIX)

The parson is to keep up with his neighbouring priests and to assist them with worship or pastoral care when appropriate. There is a strong sense of solidarity in Herbert's vision of the priesthood and a priest is always to welcome another priest into his house and to receive him as if he were the greatest of lords.

The Village

For Herbert, the priest is always a person in a specific place, the parish. The 'parish' is both a religious and a social reality. It is the community of all people who dwell in a particular place however infrequently they darken the doors of the church building. Certainly in Herbert's time and even until today in a few English rural places, the parish defined who you were. It dominated other human associations. It was the one place that you belonged to from birth to death – and even beyond death. Your ancestors' graves filled the churchyard and you might expect to be buried next to them in your turn. This 'sense of place' was intense, shaped as it was by landscape as well as social or religious ties.

In our own more urbanised, mobile and perhaps rootless culture, this vision appears to some people to offer a security that many of us lack. There may be some truth in this feeling but the results of parochialism could also be stifling. There are hints of this in Herbert when he suggests that the priest should try to encourage parishioners to have a sense of the wider Church and civic society and to honour their obligations of charity to neighbouring parishes. Herbert uses the place word 'neighbour-hood' to describe the attitude of neighbourliness that he sees as a duty and debt.

> Especially if God have sent any calamity, either by fire or famine, to any neighbouring parish, then he expects no brief; but taking his parish together *the next Sunday*, or *holy day*, and exposing them to the uncertainty of human affairs, none knowing whose turn may be next; and, then, when he hath affrighted them with this, exposing the obligation of charity and neighbourhood, he first gives himself liberally, and then incites them to give – making together a sum either to be sent, or, which were more comfortable, all together choosing some fit day to carry it themselves, and cheer the afflicted. (Chapter XIX)

It is by being located in such specific places that the priest has an identity and a role. The priest's attitude is to view the parish as his own family (Chapter XVI) and 'all his joy and thought' (Chapter XVII). He has an immense sense of responsibility for the local community because he 'is in God's stead to his parish' (Chapter XX) and his role is at the heart of the community not only as pastor but also as lawyer and physician (Chapter XXIII).

For Herbert, this vision of a 'priest in a place' is expressed most commonly in a pattern of daily visiting around the village which he describes as 'the parson in circuit' (Chapter XIV). The priest is to be present to people 'most naturally as they are'.

There is an intensity of presence in Herbert's description of the priest's life and ministry that can feel oppressive from our point of view. However, we should recall that the problem of non-resident clergy had dogged the English Church since the Middle Ages and continued to do so after the formation of a national Church of England. So 'residence' became an important ideal in any agenda for a reformed and more spiritually alert clergy. As a consequence Herbert's parson essentially commits himself to a version of the old monastic virtue of stability and only journeys outside his normal locality for 'a just occasion (which he diligently and strictly weigheth)'. There is a spiritual discipline involved in not continually seeking to escape being alongside the people a priest is called to serve.

Nation and World

Herbert has a sense of place beyond the local place of the parish and, more broadly, the diocese and the neighbourhood. Herbert is typical of his time in having a strong sense of service to his country. The parish means both church community and village. Herbert's understanding of 'nation' is also an overlap of Church and society. His priest is to bring up his children first as Christians and second as 'commonwealth's men' (sic). When he invites his neighbours to a meal he is to 'raise up their minds to apprehend God's good blessing to our Church and state' (Chapter VIII).

Although Herbert's criticism of idleness has a moral tone (Chapter XXXII), it also refers to the debt of service owed to our country. This service may be local or national. Thus the person who has some spare time and energy left after normal employment and care for the family should think of taking on some public role in the locality such as managing the woods or common land. People with 'gravity and ripeness of judgement' should consider putting themselves forwards as lay magistrates (Justices of the Peace). Herbert also suggests that to become a Member of Parliament, and to be conscientious and active there, is one of the highest duties a person can undertake for the sake of the nation. Or one might become an expert in fortification or navigation. A life in commerce is not to be sneered at especially for younger sons who might otherwise spend their days 'in dressing, complimenting, visiting, and sporting'. Finally Herbert suggests that foreign travel was a value but even here service of one's country is the main motivation. The traveller might either learn business and manufacturing skills in Europe that could be brought home or might think of serving in the new colonies in America which Herbert clearly sees as a religious as well as civil occupation.

For the modern reader, Herbert's portrayal of an overlap between Church and society, or Church and nation, raises obvious problems. Herbert accepts the notion of religious and social Establishment without questioning it. Many Christians these days would reject or at least seriously question this. Indeed, if we compare the writings of George Herbert with those of Thomas Traherne or Henry Vaughan only a few decades later, it is clear that after the terrible divisions of the Civil War Herbert's ideal of a well-ordered Church connected to a well-ordered nation was no longer easy to sustain. In contrast to Herbert, both Traherne and Vaughan, while faithful Anglicans, describe a much more inward, mystical, non-institutional spirituality.

Despite these difficulties, in other ways George Herbert's vision of an overlap of Church and civil society does have positive qualities that continue to resonate with our contemporary spiritual values. For one thing, this overlap reminds us that a holistic spirituality should be neither individualistic nor spiritualised. It necessarily has a social, public or 'civil', dimension. The overlap also emphasises a more inclusive model of the Church and of belonging (by virtue of being born into a given locality) in contrast to a more purified, gathered and therefore elite model. Equally, Herbert reminds Christians of all ages that our sense of place can become decidedly parochial. In his own modest way, Herbert points to horizons beyond the local – whether it be other communities nearby with whom we might share our abundance in their time of trial or need or whether it be service of the country and society at large. At the beginning of the third millennium spirituality rightly emphasises a much more global sense of place and community than Herbert would have understood. Yet Herbert's emphasis on the importance of locality, of the *local*, paradoxically speaks to our contemporary need in the West also to recover a sense of the small scale and the personal in a world that increasingly operates on a macro and impersonal level.

Community

Our sense of place is as closely linked to human relations as it is to physical landscapes. A vital part of Herbert's vision of 'place' concerns human and religious *community*. 'Community' is a key element of Herbert's spirituality. It is first and foremost a rooted community, based on the particular places where we may find 'home' – whether that is a family household or a village. Within Herbert's vision of community there is a careful balance of prayer, study and recreation. At the heart of it lies a strong sense of shared history that links together our sense of place and our sense of time. This is probably one reason why Herbert appears to prize so highly ancient customs as well as regularity and rhythm. Individual people find their identity by slipping into this stream of history. Religiously, this 'community history' is shaped by liturgy. This offers a rhythm for days and seasons. It allows space for the personal. Yet liturgy also insists that our stories are ultimately given meaning not only by intertwining with the stories of other people past, present and future but also by means of an encounter between all these stories and God's story in Christ. For Herbert, in liturgy *this* time and *this* place connect with all time and all places. In fact, the same may be said of the 'liturgy' of everyday actions and everyday relations in which Herbert equally believed that eternity and God could be found. Inevitably, an experience of community shaped by worship not only draws us out of ourselves but, collectively, leads the community as a whole beyond parochialism. At root, Herbert's community does not exist simply to reflect the preoccupations of its own place or to service its own concerns. True Christian community is a place of hospitality and also a place out of which comes a strong sense of service.

6

Christian Discipleship and a Holy Life

One of the most important threads that runs through Herbert's poems is a personal relationship with God characterised by struggle both on the part of God and on that of the human heart. The intensity of the poems suggests that the struggle they describe was a real and personal one rather than something merely contrived although I have already indicated that their purpose was not autobiographical but to evoke a deepening of the reader's own relationship with God. The words attributed by Isaak Walton to Herbert concerning his writings accord well with the substance of the poems themselves. Herbert sent the poems from his deathbed to his friend Nicholas Ferrar. The message that accompanied them apparently suggested that the poems were 'a picture of the many spiritual conflicts that have passed betwixt God and my soul before I could subject mine to the will of Jesus my Master: in whose service I have now found perfect freedom'.

The poems themselves, however, do not chart a simple spiritual path, for example the classical progression from purgative way to unitive way or some equivalent. Complexity and simplicity, doubt and faith vie with each other throughout. Even the final poem of the central section of *The Temple,* 'Love III', continues to express a deep spiritual struggle. Despite the apparent resolution and surrender expressed in the last line, there is an ambiguity that suggests that such surrenders are never finally conclusive on this side of death. It is only the latest of several such surrenders throughout the poems.

> Love bade me welcome: yet my soul drew back,
>> Guilty of dust and sin.
> But quick-ey'd Love, observing me grow slack
>> From my first entrance in,
> Drew nearer to me, sweetly questioning,
>> If I lacked anything.
>
> A guest, I answer'd, worthy to be here:
>> Love said, You shall be he.
> I the unkind, ungrateful? Ah my dear,
>> I cannot look on thee.
> Love took my hand, and smiling did reply,
>> Who made the eyes but I?
>
> Truth Lord, but I have marr'd them: let my shame
>> Go where it doth deserve.
> And know you not, says Love, who bore the blame?
>> My dear, then I will serve.
> You must sit down, says Love, and taste my meat:
>> So I did sit and eat.

In fact, the poems of the middle section of *The Temple* as a whole chart a fluctuating relationship with God in which God struggles with Herbert's 'peevish heart' ('Sion', line 13).

Inner Struggle

It is impossible to focus the nature of Herbert's inner struggle towards spiritual freedom on one key theme. Structurally, the poems seem to offer a sense of movement from a more moral, active, meditative stance in 'The Church Porch', the first section of *The Temple*, to a more God-centred, contemplative and passive mood at the end of 'The Church'. However, if there is indeed a movement towards contemplative experience it also involves more complex spiritual movements. Herbert's theology of the human person suggests that humanity is both the meeting place of heaven and earth and a place of conflict,

> A wonder tortur'd in the space
> Betwixt this world and that of grace.
>
> ('Affliction IV')

I would summarise Herbert's struggle as a battle to accept God's love but this covers a variety of sub-plots. In *The Spiritual Exercises* Ignatius Loyola suggests that the fundamental sin that separates humanity from God is pride and that spiritual freedom, therefore, consists in knowing our sinfulness and accepting the way of humility and poverty, whether spiritual or material. This view is obviously historically and socially conditioned as is Herbert's. By contrast, Herbert's basic problem initially appears as a more classically 'Protestant' sense of unworthiness and inability to cope with the single-mindedness of God's love. On further reflection, however, pride is clearly part of Herbert's struggle as well. Even in that final poem, 'Love III', Herbert shows every sign of wanting to be worthy. What is lacking at Love's feast? 'A guest, I answer'd, worthy to be here.' The fundamental question throughout the central section of *The Temple* is how the writer is to allow God to love and serve him. How is Herbert to surrender his own standards? This is a subtle form of pride but pride none the less.

Such difficulties would be a good subject for Ignatius Loyola's 'Rules for the Discernment of Spirits' aimed at the spiritually more mature person. Here temptations are not crude but masquerade 'under the guise of good' (*The Spiritual Exercises*, sections 328–36). It seems good to be worthy and to desire to be worthy. However, in reality that is to place the human capacity to respond to God at the heart of the matter rather than God's gift of love. Herbert does not deny that we are called to respond to God but the response is, paradoxically, to accept our inability to offer true love in return for true love.

It would be strange if Herbert's aristocratic sensibilities had no further impact after his conversion. It is one thing to renounce a career in public life and quite another to accept the full consequences. A number of poems express frustration and the temptation to give up. 'Affliction I' suggests the writer can see no sense in what is happening in his relationship with God.

> Well, I will change the service, and go seek
> > Some other master out.

As if to underline that there is no simple progression in our spiritual pilgrimage, a much later poem 'The Collar' has similar sentiments.

> I struck the board, and cried, No more.
> > I will abroad.
> What? Shall I ever sigh and pine?

Its dramatic form indicates the continuing temptation to

rebellion. Herbert seems to be raging against his own imperfections but behind this lies a degree of self-serving. The initial response is not surrender but revolt against the ultimate renunciation of self that seems to be required.

The endings of both 'Affliction' and 'The Collar' suggest that nothing more is asked of us than a simple acceptance of God's love. This battle to accept that God is love rather than more logically a judge is another dimension of Herbert's struggle. God confounds our reasonable expectations. We are sinners and utterly unworthy; logically we should be condemned.

> Oh dreadful Justice, what a fright and terror
> Wast thou of old,
> When sin and error
> Did show and shape thy looks to me,
> And through their glass discolour thee!

No doubt the poem 'Justice II' expresses a contrast both between the Old Law and the New Law of Christ and between the New Law and Herbert's own experience. The point is that fear belongs to the past and it is broadly true that Herbert does not appear to battle with an existential fear of God even while he struggles to accept that God *ought* not to be feared.

Herbert's struggle with God and the movement towards spiritual freedom is just as real as it is, in a somewhat different guise, in Catholic Reformation writings such as those by Ignatius Loyola. Although the will of God is central to Herbert, the dominant image for God's way of being and acting is Love. The spiritual dynamic, therefore, cannot be one of salvation simply *imposed* on human beings from outside rather than operating from within their lives and experience. God's love is conclusively and freely offered. It is not provisionally on offer depending on our capacity to earn it. After Christ, there is nothing more to be achieved or completed in salvation. Such a view is equally true of the 'Protestant' Herbert and the 'Catholic' Ignatius Loyola. Yet, equally, both recognise that God's love has to be truly received.

In the poem 'Redemption' Herbert employs the imagery of tenants and leases. The poet as 'tenant' seeks to 'make a suit' to God in heaven as the 'rich Lord' requesting that he be given a new lease as the old was no longer satisfactory. When he finds the Lord it is not in heaven but strangely on earth amidst thieves and murderers. The suit is immediately granted on sight without more discussion. This conclusion has sometimes been read as teaching that a human search for God is ultimately meaningless from the point of view of Reformed theology. However, this mistakes the poem's own dynamism. The central point of the poem is not that seeking God is valueless but that God in Christ is not to be found in the expected place. The writer 'knowing his great birth' sought God

> . . . in great resorts;
> In cities, theatres, gardens, parks and courts:

In fact God is found among the unworthy and powerless. This provides a salutary lesson to the poet who, it seems, struggles with such a notion. God grants the suit from within the messiness of the human condition, not from the safety of power and invulnerability.

Thus, it is the case in 'Redemption', as it is in the poem 'Love', that nothing is imposed but everything is granted. God is revealed as the one who respects the human person. The final surrender of the poet in the poem 'Love' – 'You must sit down, says Love, and taste my meat:/ So I did sit and eat' – is neither hopeless resignation nor the act of someone who obeys an order.

It is the acceptance of an invitation. In that acceptance is freedom. This is because it involves, too, the realisation that in the invitation to eat Love's meat 'I the unkind, ungrateful' have been granted a true vision of my real value before God.

Both the Catholic reformer Ignatius Loyola in *The Spiritual Exercises* and George Herbert in *The Temple* begin with human unworthiness. Although they use a different spiritual language, both of them map out a comparable pilgrimage of the human spirit. This journey involves a realisation that human beings do not ever cease to be unworthy but are actually loved by God *as sinners*. Any authentic following of Christ begins with that realisation. Interestingly, both spiritual teachers bring their map of the spiritual pilgrimage to a climax with a contemplation of God's love that brings with it a recognition that it is God who gives all and achieves all.

> Take, Lord, and receive all my liberty, my memory, my understanding and my whole will, all that I have and possess. You gave it to me; to you Lord I return it. Everything is yours; dispose of it according to your will. Give me your love and your grace for they are enough for me. (*The Spiritual Exercises*, section 235)

The Calling of Discipleship: A Holy Life

For Herbert, there is a close link between the demands of discipleship and Christian service and between service and personal holiness. Nowhere is this made more explicit than in his treatise *The Country Parson*. Although this concerns the life of the priest, it is not difficult to see that the fundamental values that are portrayed are those of Christian discipleship in a broader sense.

There is a totality to Herbert's portrayal of the priest. His emphasis on personal holiness serves to underline that to be a pastor is not merely a job but a way of life. It involves every moment and every aspect of life including how the priest spends money or takes leisure (Chapter III), behaves courteously, gives charitably or offers hospitality (Chapters XI and XII) and even how he manages his own household and family (Chapter X). To be effective in pastoral service involves considerable spiritual struggle (Chapter XXXIII) and Herbert's ideal pastor continually strives to become 'an absolute master and commander of himself, for all the purposes which God hath ordained him' (Chapter III). Yet, despite Herbert's rather traditional emphasis on mortification, he is quite clear that it is more important to observe the spirit rather than purely the letter of ascetical practices such as fasting. This is particularly true if the person is physically weak (Chapter X). No doubt Herbert's sensitivity refers to his own experience of poor health which (according to a letter to his mother) had led him while a student at Cambridge to have to supplement the traditional Lenten fare.

Herbert recommended that the parson should be fed by intellectual pursuits. 'The country parson hath read the Fathers also, and the schoolmen and the later writers, or a good proportion of all' (Chapter V). Yet at the heart of the parson's pastoral ministry lies holiness, or what we might term 'spirituality'. Without this nothing counts. So 'The Parson's Library' (Chapter XXXIII) does not in fact refer to a collection of books. 'The country parson's library is a holy life.'

The notion that the roots of the priest's ministry lie in a holy life also applies to the parson's preaching. The attention of the listeners is gained

> first, by choosing texts of devotion, not controversy, moving and ravishing texts, whereof the Scriptures are full. Secondly, by dipping and seasoning all our words and sentences in our hearts, before they come into our mouths, truly affecting and cordially expressing all that we say; so that the auditors may plainly perceive that every word is heart-deep.
> (Chapter VII)

The priest's eloquence consists not so much in verbal eloquence as in 'holiness' in the sense of an experiential and transformative engagement with God and God's Word. Herbert's parson is effective as a preacher to the degree that his life is a window through which God's grace can pour onto the community.

> Lord, how can man preach thy eternal word?
> He is a brittle crazy glass:
> Yet in thy temple thou dost him afford
> This glorious and transcendent place,
> To be a window, through thy grace.
>
> But when thou dost anneal in glass thy story,
> Making thy life to shine within
> The holy preacher's; then the light and glory
> More rev'rend grows, and more doth win:
> Which else shows wat'rish, bleak and thin.
>
> ('The Windows')

Herbert's view of the 'holiness' of the minister or priest is somewhat ambiguous. In general, a thoroughly Protestant viewpoint tended to reject the medieval hierarchy of vocations – and especially the notion of a special priestly caste. However, in its search for balance, the Elizabethan Settlement left the Church of England with significant elements of the older model of a distinctive priesthood.

Herbert stresses the vocational nature of every human life under God. Herbert's country parson is to respect and nurture the vocation of everyone. From the time of creation, all human beings have had a 'calling' and that continues to remain true. 'All are either to have a calling, or prepare for it' (Chapter XXXII). The parson is not to despise the 'holiness' of the most lowly of people or the most ordinary of places.

> He holds the rule, that nothing is little in God's service: If it once have the honour of that Name, it grows great instantly. Wherefore neither disdaineth he to enter into the poorest cottage, though he even creep into it, and though it smell never so loathsomely. For both God is there also, and those for whom God died. (Chapter XIV)

Whether in the parson's own life or in the life of parishioners, the ordinary daily round and the everyday world is the common context for God's presence and action.

> Teach me, my God and King,
> In all things thee to see,
> And what I do in any thing,
> To do it as for thee:
>> ('The Elixir')

Yet, alongside an emphasis on the common Christian calling, Herbert also retained elements of a pre-Reformation view of the particularity of the ordained ministry. Article XXXII of the 1562 Articles of Religion made it clear that clergy might equally marry or remain single 'at their own discretion'. Although the 'meaning' of clerical celibacy varies according to historical and even geographical context, it is certainly the case that celibacy stands for a great deal more than mere sexual abstinence. A complete spirituality of lifestyle is implied by that particular boundary. Herbert's personal view of the best possible lifestyle for the priest seems to have been somewhat more tightly drawn. He allows that for pragmatic reasons it may be best for the priest to marry yet 'The country parson considering that virginity is a higher state than matrimony, and that the ministry requires the best and highest things, is rather unmarried, than married' (Chapter IX). Interestingly, this somewhat unreformed aspect of Herbert's idealised portrait of the priest is rarely if ever commented upon. The apparent preference of Queen Elizabeth I for a celibate clergy at the time of the religious Settlement appears to have sustained sympathy for this viewpoint in parts of the Church of England until the end of the Stuart era.

George Herbert paints a quasi-monastic portrait of the celibate priest. 'He spends his days in fasting and prayer' (Chapter IX). Indeed, Herbert recommends that the priest should go beyond the minimum required by Church law. The priest is to add 'some other days for fasting and hours for prayer'. Interestingly, it is to early desert asceticism that Herbert turns for inspiration. 'He [the priest] often readeth the lives of the primitive monks, hermits and virgins.'

Having said that Herbert retains something of the more traditional Catholic view of the spirituality of priesthood, this comment needs to be qualified to some degree. In the Church of England, priesthood did not exist in theological or spiritual isolation from a relationship to a specific community. The Church of England spirituality of priesthood is not a substitute for the call to holiness of the whole community. Priesthood therefore has a more exemplary quality. Herbert would surely have understood his comments on celibacy and on the ascetic life of the priest to be some kind of lesson on the cost of discipleship offered to all baptised Christians.

Effectiveness and integrity in leading public worship was intimately connected to the pastor's own spiritual depths (Chapters VI and VIII). For Herbert, there is a particular intimacy between God and those who preside at the Holy Communion and this lays a considerable burden upon them.

> The country parson being to administer the Sacraments, is at a stand with himself, how or what behaviour to assume for so holy things. Especially at Communion times he is in a great confusion, as being not only to receive God, but to break, and administer him.
>
> (Chapter XXII 'The Parson in Sacraments')

The priesthood is a 'Blest Order, which in power dost so excel'.

> But th' holy men of God such vessels are,
> As serve him up, who all the world commands:
> When God vouchsafeth to become our fare,
> Their hands convey him who conveys their hands.
> Oh what pure things, most pure must those things be,
> Who bring my God to me!
>
> ('The Priesthood')

Yet the gap between this awesome calling and frail human nature, sin and failings, is vast. A person can only respond to the call to priesthood in full knowledge of unworthiness. The poem 'Aaron' plays with the image of dress, inward and outer, no doubt with an eye to questions of priestly vestments. The true Aaron has

> Holiness on the head,
> Light and perfections on the breast.

Yet this is not so in the 'poor priest' (Herbert perhaps) who is naturally 'drest' in profaneness, defects and passions.

The only answer to our unworthiness is to 'put on Christ' for 'In him I am well drest'. What we wear is 'sacramental'. Outward vesture is the sign of inward grace and of a body and soul in harmony. The symbolic putting on of vestments by the priest is for Herbert an illustration of the way Christians must put on Christ. This spiritual 'vesture' both covers our unworthiness and at the same time portrays our dignity as God's creatures and our vocation to service-centred love.

> Christ is my only head,
> My alone only heart and breast,
> My only music, striking me ev'n dead;
> That to the old man I may rest,
> And be in him new drest.

7

Prayer: The Soul in Paraphrase

For George Herbert, the nature of God is ultimately beyond the power of human words to express. This is another aspect of Herbert's sense of the essentially elusive and hidden quality of God. Words may serve to describe and to praise but if we rely on them too much (as noted in the poem 'Jordan II') they merely shut us off from the ultimate source of light and life. For this reason, Herbert may have placed a high value on preaching but he had a still higher estimation of prayer. Even in *The Country Parson*, where there is a fairly didactic model of ministry, 'the Country Parson preacheth constantly' but not primarily in a catechetical way. He is to choose 'texts of Devotion, not Controversy, moving and ravishing texts, whereof the Scriptures are full' (Chapter VII). The purpose of preaching is to lead people to prayer for 'Praying's the end of preaching' ('Perirrhanterium', line 410). And if prayer for Herbert is above all 'the Church's banquet', the prayer of the Church, the daily Offices and the Eucharist, there is beyond those structures and set formulae a promise of something ultimately intangible; a way of knowing that is perhaps mystical. This is expressed beautifully yet allusively in the accumulated images of 'Prayer II'. Prayer is 'the soul's blood', the very source of life within us. It is also 'the soul in paraphrase': the essence of our true self.

The Eucharist

I have already hinted at the importance of the Eucharist for Herbert's spirituality. As we shall see later in this chapter, the poem 'Prayer I' includes distinctly eucharistic allusions. The Eucharist is at the heart of Herbert's spiritual sensibilities and consequently features regularly throughout his poetry. The poem on 'The Holy Communion' within the collection *The Temple* is far less explicitly theological, at least in the sense of apologetics, than another poem of the same name. Herbert settles not simply theologically but spiritually for the mysterious, or mystical nature of the Eucharist whose powerful reality is beyond the powers of human definition.

Although Herbert does not become deeply embroiled in polemical argument about the Eucharist, it is possible to gain a feel for what he believes. Throughout the poems he regularly uses words associated with the presence of Christ, the heavenly realm, the intersection of time and eternity, the banquet of the kingdom and the Eucharist as the medium for God's mystical union with us. The central section of the poems, 'The Church', is immediately preceded by the final poem of 'The Church Porch', entitled 'Superliminary', where we are enjoined

> . . . approach, and taste
> The church's mystical repast.

This leads into the very first poem of the main section, 'The Altar', where the eucharistic references could not be clearer. This in turn is followed by 'The Sacrifice' with its strong emphasis on Christ's saving passion and resonances of the old liturgy of Holy Week. As a good Protestant, Herbert's theology of the

Eucharist emphasised that through it we are brought to share in all the benefits of the passion. But then, we are now more aware that this is good Catholic theology as well. At the other end of this central section is the poem 'Love III' which suggests both the celebration of the Eucharist within time and the heavenly banquet beyond time and the connections between the two. The final words,

> You must sit down, says Love, and taste my meat:
> So I did sit and eat.

are followed by the opening words of the *Gloria in Excelsis Deo* which act as a Post-Communion prayer in Cranmer's Prayer Book. Although the spiritual teaching of 'The Church' has several dimensions, its dynamic structure clearly seems to be conceived in terms of the Eucharist, the heart of the Church's life.

Methods of Prayer

Our contemporary instincts tend to make us concerned to learn about particular techniques of prayer or meditation. Herbert's *The Country Parson* makes some reference to private prayer (for example, Chapter X 'The Parson in his House' and Chapter XXXI 'The Parson in Liberty') but there is very little explicit teaching on ways of praying. Most of what can be drawn from Herbert is present only implicitly.

An important element of Herbert's teaching on prayer is his insistence on the importance of a daily pattern and on its connection with everyday life. Members of the parson's household are recommended to pray when they rise in the morning and before they go to sleep. The parson should also teach his parishioners that prayer twice a day, every day (and more on Sundays) is 'necessary' for all Christians. In the context of the priest's own prayers, Chapter VIII suggests that the morning prayers should request God to bless the work of the day and evening prayer should request God to accept the work of the day and to pardon any faults. In many respects, the poems 'Mattins' and 'Evensong' offer much the same focus about prayer at either end of the day. In traditional devotional language, Herbert recommends a kind of 'morning offering' and a self-examination, or examination of conscience, in the evening. As we have already seen, a form of examination of conscience is also recommended in 'The Church Porch'. A prayerful confession of faults is also hinted at in the poem 'The Method'. There are also references to praying at all times (perhaps including ejaculatory prayer) in *The Country Parson*, Chapter XXXV. The value of petitionary prayer is mentioned in several places and there are particular allusions to it in the poem, 'Prayer III'. Finally, the chapter 'The Parson Praying' in *The Country Parson* suggests that people may be taught to make their own personal meditations in the pauses between the words and phrases of public prayer.

The strength of Herbert's concern to teach the importance of daily prayer fits well with his overall concern to teach a spirituality that is connected to everyday life and which values even the smallest events and details as contexts for meeting and responding to God. Interestingly, in *The Country Parson*, Chapter XXXI, Herbert seems to recommend a more monastic pattern of daily prayer for those people he calls 'the Godly'. This more intense pattern would add 'some hours of prayer, as at nine, or at three, or at midnight, or as they think fit'. Herbert refers to the long-standing tradition of these 'additionary' prayers which may imply some historical sense of pre-Reformation monastic or collegiate patterns. However, it is just as likely that Herbert was thinking of his contemporary Nicholas Ferrar and the pattern at the Little Gidding community where a form of family monasticism was practised.

The poems of *The Temple* are themselves predominantly devotional. Indeed, many of them are conversations of great intensity between Herbert and God. As his poem 'The Quiddity' makes clear, Herbert understood poetry itself to be a form of prayer.

> My God, a verse is not a crown
> ... But it is that which while I use
> I am with thee, and *Most take all.*

The conversational poems of 'The Church' are similar to the style of intimate prayer that Ignatius Loyola and other spiritual teachers of the Catholic Reformation recommended and described as 'Colloquies'.

> A colloquy is made, properly speaking, in the way one friend speaks to another, or a servant to one in authority – now begging a favour, now accusing oneself of some misdeed, now telling one's concerns and asking counsel about them.
>
> (*Spiritual Exercises*, section 54)

Many of Herbert's poems are meditations with strong biblical references and from 'The Parson's Knowledge' in *The Country Parson* it is clear that Herbert himself must have been familiar with the concept of biblical meditation although no precise method is indicated.

The question arises as to whether Herbert shows any awareness of more contemplative forms of prayer. Once again, he certainly does not offer any explicit teaching. However, a strong sense of contemplative awareness and experience shines through a number of poems – a kind of awareness that inspired the composer Vaughan Williams to call his George Herbert song cycle 'Mystical Songs'. The poem sometimes titled 'Prayer II', and sometimes listed as the second part of the preceding 'The Holy Communion', suggests that prayer has the capacity to transport us from this time and space to heaven and to the kind of relationship with God that Adam once knew before the Fall.

> He might to heav'n from Paradise go,
>> As from one room t'another.

In one of the poems set to music by the composer Vaughan Williams, 'Easter' (sometimes divided into I and II), there are hints of the writer being transported to another level of awareness where all time is caught up into the eternal present of Christ's Easter triumph. In another of the 'Mystical Songs', 'The Call', an intensity of experience is expressed that is beyond the conventional.

> Come, my Way, my Truth, my Life:
> Such a Way, as gives us breath:
> Such a Truth, as ends all strife:
> And such a Life, as killeth death.

> Come, my Light, my Feast, my Strength:
> Such a Light, as shows a feast:
> Such a Feast, as mends in length:
> Such a Strength, as makes his guest.

> Come, my Joy, my Love, my Heart:
> Such a Joy, as none can move:

> Such a Love, as none can part:
> Such a Heart, as joys in love.

The same intensity of spiritual intimacy and presence is evident in the poem 'Love III' already quoted and which apparently provoked some kind of mystical experience in Simone Weil.

The Poem 'Prayer I'

Some of the most striking lines of Herbert concerning prayer occur in the first poem of that name in *The Temple*. This is an extraordinary poem even in its construction. It is a sonnet with no main verb but with a succession of metaphors tumbling one after another. The lines need to be read aloud as their impact on our understanding of prayer relies on a cumulative effect rather than on a conclusive definition or progressive argument. In attempting to express the nature of prayer, Herbert turns away from the obvious path of simile: 'prayer is like . . .' Metaphor provides a much greater imaginative scope that enables him to entice the reader beyond the limits of the expressible. Paradoxically, therefore, Herbert offers many images of prayer and yet also suggests an underlying truth that prayer cannot ultimately be described. It is a mysterious process that enables us to touch ultimate Mystery. Herbert's range of metaphors swings between time and eternity, the everyday and heaven, in just the same way that prayer forms a bridge between two worlds.

> Prayer the Church's banquet, Angel's age,
> God's breath in man returning to his birth,
> The soul in paraphrase, heart in pilgrimage,
> The Christian plummet sounding heav'n and earth;

Engine against th' Almighty, sinner's tower,
    Reversed thunder, Christ-side-piercing spear,
    The six-days world transposing in an hour,
A kind of tune, which all things hear and fear;
Softness and peace, and joy, and love, and bliss,
    Exalted Manna, gladness of the best,
    Heaven in ordinary, man well drest,
The milky way, the bird of Paradise,
    Church-bells beyond the stars heard, the soul's
      blood,
    The land of spices; something understood.

The poem begins with the phrase 'the Church's banquet'. As we might expect in Herbert's spirituality, all prayer is to be understood as common prayer, the prayer of the Church. The metaphor has another dimension as well. A banquet is a meal. Prayer is our spiritual food – a metaphor deepened by the use of further metaphors later in the poem, 'exalted manna' and 'land of spices'. It is very likely that the opening words also allude to the Eucharist that Herbert understood as the heart of Christian prayer. The term 'heavenly banquet' was Richard Hooker's preferred eucharistic metaphor and Herbert's own poem 'The Banquet' and his banquet imagery elsewhere in the collection (for example, in 'Love III') are eucharistic in tone.

Prayer is not merely 'in common', however. It is also deeply personal. Prayer is 'the soul's blood', the very source of life coursing through us. It is also 'the soul in paraphrase': it expands the soul to its full potential and is the most perfect expression of our inner self, our deepest self. 'God's breath in man returning to his birth' suggests that prayer has the capacity to return us to the first moment of creation, to the very source of life itself, to a relationship with God that mirrors the experience of Paradise.

The richness of the imagery throughout the poem and its sensuous quality may give the impression that prayer is merely 'softness and peace, and joy, and love, and bliss'. However, hints of spiritual struggle save the poem from feeling unrealistic and out of touch with the complexity and, at times, confusion of our own experiences of spiritual journeying. For most of the time on our spiritual journey we simply cannot see 'the land of spices' nor hear the 'Church-bells beyond the stars'. It is fine to write of 'softness and peace, and love, and joy, and bliss'. But our own inner moods vary and there is, therefore, an unknown quality to our journeying. 'Engine against th' Almighty'. Prayer lays siege to God. This is an ambiguous image that suggests both perseverance and combat. The poem admits that sometimes there is conflict on our journey. We actually battle with God as we struggle to know how our heart's desire and what we sometimes call the will of God may be brought together – may come to be realised as one thing. Herbert is not afraid to admit this. In the poem 'Artillery' he says to God,

> Then we are shooters both, and Thou dost deign
> To enter combat with us, and contest
> With thine own clay.

In this sense of spiritual combat and struggle with God, Herbert not only echoes the emotional tone of the Book of Psalms that was such a favourite of his but also a long history of Christian spirituality from early desert monasticism onwards. Sometimes, however, the journey is all there is and so we move trustingly along the road as best we can.

'Heart in pilgrimage'. In our commitment to prayer, George

Herbert came to understand that the depths of a person, 'the heart', could be radically changed. Underlying our human journey is an experience of transformation whereby fear of God's wrath gives way to a deep realisation of God's loving acceptance of us in Christ. In Christ, our stony hearts may yield gradually to the wooing of God's love. The graphic metaphor, 'Christ-side-piercing spear' reminds us of similar imagery in another poem, 'The Bag'. The wound in Christ's side becomes a space where we may safely deposit our messages that Christ then bears to God. Herbert's Christ-centred spirituality may also be at the heart of the words 'man well drest'. The phrase recalls the poem 'Aaron' where the priest is properly vested when he is caught up into the life of Christ,

> . . . my only head,
> My alone only heart and breast,
> My only music . . .

It is in union with Christ that all Christians become 'well drest'.

Yet, in the midst of the struggle and the journey, Herbert always had a profound sense that the world of everyday experience and of nature was filled with the presence of God. Through its powerful and cumulative use of images, the poem 'Prayer' offers an extraordinarily rich vision of the sacred, of God, as something we may encounter within the ordinary and yet which carries us beyond the ordinary. Natural and biblical allusions combine with strikingly original images ('Church-bells beyond the stars heard') to suggest that the mundane, the daily, the everyday are transfigured by the radiance of divine glory. 'Heaven in ordinary'. Interestingly, an 'ordinary' in Herbert's time could also mean the regular menu of fairly cheap food listed in an inn or it might mean the part of the inn where the common menu was served or even the kind of people who normally ate such meals in such a place. Perhaps there are echoes here of the poem 'Redemption' where God, the 'rich Lord', is found not 'in great resorts' but amongst the 'ragged noise and mirth' made by the kinds of somewhat disreputable people who might inhabit the common dining room of a seventeenth-century inn!

In prayer, it is possible for us to be transported, even if momentarily, to another realm entirely. The metaphors 'Angel's age', 'the milky way' and a tune that is 'beyond the stars' suggest that prayer enables us to pass beyond the limits of human frailty. Prayer touches infinity and immortality. Herbert's careful phrasing appears to suggest a certain reciprocity in the relationship between heaven and earth. The ambiguous metaphor 'Church-bells beyond the stars heard' suggests both that the music of heaven becomes accessible to us and that the music of our lives and prayer enriches the life of heaven.

'The six-days world transposing in an hour'. In prayer we may be drawn into a sense of the ordinary transfigured – not in the sense of left behind or rejected but seen in another light. Or maybe it is better to stay with Herbert's own love of musical imagery that appears on so many occasions throughout his poetry. After all, the next line suggests that prayer is 'a kind of tune'. Prayer *transposes* the six-days world into another key. The world has its music but in the experience of prayer and meditation the human heart becomes more fully attuned to a deeper reality behind the surface impressions and so, to continue a musical metaphor, what is heard is pitched differently. Prayer is also 'The Christian plummet sounding heav'n and earth' – something weighty that, as it were, we drop down to test the depths and authenticity of our lives and experiences. A plummet enables us to realise that there *are* depths and that there is a truth in those depths that we sometimes scarcely sense.

For George Herbert, in prayer we come as close to the reality we call 'God' as we can in this phase of our existence. In the poem 'Prayer I', the 'now' and the 'not yet' of our human lives continually intersect. We are drawn to reach out beyond the immediate and yet it is in and through the immediate that we may hear the music beyond the stars and glimpse the land of spices in the here and now. Yet as our lives are at present, there is always something tentative and provisional about this experience. We have not yet reached the end of our journey. There is not yet a final harmony.

The poem concludes with that pregnant but elusive phrase, 'something understood'. In the end, all attempts to describe prayer fail. The final metaphor is a paradoxical climax to the poem because it leaves us not with a definition – in fact not with a conclusion at all. It is deliberately open-ended. In the experience of prayer and meditation there is '*something* understood'. The 'understanding' is not intellectual or objective knowledge but is something that is available to those who expose themselves to the risks of love. It is tentative and it is incomplete. So this 'something' deepens our desire and presses us onwards so that we cannot remain content with 'this' and 'that' when our nature ultimately makes us to want *all*. And all, in the end, means God. In that something we may sense on the margins of our awareness the hope and promise of a final resolution, the ultimate seeing and hearing that Herbert's poem celebrates.

> Church-bells beyond the stars heard, the soul's blood,
> The land of spices; something understood.

8

A Spirituality of Service

'There is no greater sign of holiness, than the procuring, and rejoicing in another's good' (*The Country Parson*, Chapter VII). The service of other people is a central feature of George Herbert's spirituality. His essentially pastoral purpose is implicit throughout his writings even in the way that the poetic collection *The Temple* is structured. It is also made explicit in a few individual poems. However, Herbert gives greatest attention to a spirituality of service in the prose essay on the nature of priesthood-discipleship, *The Country Parson*. It is impossible to ignore the fact that, in the religious and social context of his times, Herbert inevitably views pastoral service as mainly the role of the ordained. But not exclusively. Herbert hints that a spirituality of service is part of the wider Christian vocation when he suggests a role for members of the priest's family and household in visiting the sick, in the healing ministry and above all in spiritual conversation. In our modern context, it would not be invalid to reread Herbert's spirituality of service as relevant to the whole people of God except where it clearly applies to ordained ministry.

A spirituality of service places the care of other people at the centre of a Christian's life. In Herbert's own terms, care is not simply about specific actions but something that involves the whole person of the priest or Christian. The sorrows, joys, grief and glories of the parish become those of the country parson. To serve is to act as an agent of reconciliation, to visit the sick and to exhort others to a life of grace. For a Christian, the pursuit of spirituality cannot be separated from a call to serve others. To be holy is to share oneself with others. Interestingly, the English writer on mysticism, Evelyn Underhill, suggested that service of others was one of the most characteristic signs of a Christian mystic. She noted that the greatest Christian mystics such as Bernard of Clairvaux or Teresa of Avila also poured their lives out in the service of other people. George Herbert was convinced that the one thing that mattered for a Christian was to worship God in spirit and truth, living always in a spirit of repentance. However, the process of living this out inevitably overflows into a service of others.

To be pastoral is to be God's 'watchman' (*The Country Parson*, Chapter XVIII), to be in God's place and to help to discharge God's promises (Chapter XX). More particularly, a spirituality of service or pastoral care is Christ-centred. The pastor is the deputy of Christ (Chapter I) to continue his work of reconciliation. A spirituality of service finds its strength in imitation of Christ. It is necessary, though difficult, for the pastor 'to put on the profound humility, and the exact temperance of our Lord Jesus' (Chapter IX).

> It's true, we cannot reach Christ's forti'th day;
> Yet to go part of that religious way,
> Is better than to rest:
> We cannot reach our Saviour's purity;
> Yet we are bid, *Be holy ev'n as he.*
> In both let's do our best.

Who goeth in the way which Christ hath gone,
Is much more sure to meet with him, than one
That travelleth byways:
Perhaps my God, though he be far before,
May turn, and take me by the hand, and more
May strengthen my decays.

('Lent', ll. 31–42)

For the pastor,

Christ is my only head,
My alone only heart and breast,
My only music . . .
My doctrine tun'd by Christ.

('Aaron')

The Ecclesial Context

We have already seen that seventeenth-century Anglican spirituality as a whole is overtly focused on the life of the Church.
Herbert's approach to preaching and teaching is always within
an ecclesial context. For him, the Church serves because God
serves and because the Church serves the pastor serves. If the
parson is 'the deputy of Christ', he is also and always the rep-
resentative of the Church as Herbert indicates in his comments
on the importance of using the official Catechism (Chapters V
and XXI).

Equally, just as preaching should lead to prayer, so one
important dimension of Herbert's overall teaching is pre-

paration for the liturgy and the sacraments of the Church, especially the Eucharist. The parson

> applies himself with catechizings, and lively exhortations, not on the Sunday of the Communion only (for then it is too late) but the Sunday, or Sundays before the Communion, or on the Eves of all those days.
>
> (Chapter XXII 'The Parson in Sacraments')

Herbert shared with people like Bishop Lancelot Andrewes and Archbishop Laud the aim of renewing the whole of society through the agency of the Church. The teaching and sacraments of the Church gather people together as agents of renewal and commitment as much in the nation as in the Church itself. Thus, Herbert's approach to service is not simply directed towards the individual person in isolation. All service in the model of Christ is to build up the community. Herbert has a very social and collective understanding of human nature.

Herbert belonged to an age when society at large and the nation were considered appropriate contexts for a vocation of service. The parson himself is 'to do his Country true and laudable service, when occasion requires' (Chapter XIX). More importantly he is to nurture a sense of service to the commonwealth in others (Chapter XXXII). Service of a person's own locality is the most immediate duty. Herbert teaches a general principle that the higher a person's status the greater the duty of service. The children in a family are to be brought up to share the sense of service of their parents. Herbert's own experience of serving as a Member of Parliament appears strongly in his very positive view of that institution and of the possibility of serving one's country within it.

In some respects, of course, Herbert's vision of society is very dated from our contemporary point of view. Although he sought to *renew* society he had no sense of the need to criticise the political or social status quo. He is somewhat childlike in his belief in the generally good order of the State. If we consider that a bitter civil war was only a decade or so ahead, we cannot avoid the impression that Herbert shared some of the blindness of the upper classes into which he was born. However, even if there is nothing in Herbert that is the equivalent of what today would be called a spirituality of justice, he is not without a certain capacity for prophetic criticism. He recognises the temptation among clergy to ingratiate themselves with the rich and powerful and is robust in his criticism of such tendencies. If priests fail to reprove the powerful when appropriate,

> they . . . while they remember their earthly Lord do much forget their heavenly; they wrong the Priesthood, neglect their duty, and shall be so far from that which they seek with their oversubmissiveness, and cringings, that they shall ever be despised. (Chapter II)

Despite these attitudes, there is still something to be learned from Herbert in today's world when the notion of 'public service' meets with an understandable degree of cynicism. If society is to be renewed at depth, we need to recover something of Herbert's view of the vocational possibilities of public life and of his sense that service is not to be confined to friends, family or to a protected world of Christian communities.

Charity

At the heart of Herbert's spirituality of service lies the classic Christian virtue of charity, *caritas* or love. 'The Country Parson is full of Charity; it is his predominant element' (Chapter XII). Insofar as charity involves giving some material assistance to those in need, the priest, and by extension every Christian, is to do this from personal possessions so that charity actually costs something. Indeed, the priest should take every opportunity of 'exposing the obligation of Charity' to his parishioners particularly when he invites them to see the neediness of people beyond the boundaries of their own village (Chapter XIX).

There is a very old-fashioned and unattractive feel to Herbert's notion that charity should aim to make people dependent! If the means is very questionable, the end is not necessarily so. For charity should be a sermon that leads people to praise God more and to take pains with their vocation.

Herbert's remarks on charity should be read in the context of his belief in the importance of courtesy. In one sense, material charity to the poor is another form of what Herbert calls a 'debt' of courtesy. In some cases, courtesy is expressed in hospitality and Herbert is quite clear that the priest should not hesitate to have the poor to dinner and to serve them personally. However, it may be that such hospitality is not what they need most. True courtesy may mean that we have to let needy people decide for themselves what they most need rather than impose our desires upon them. Thus, the money that might be used to offer poor people good food might be better employed if it were given to the poor themselves to be used by them 'to their own advantage, and suitably to their needs' (Chapter XI).

The open purse is a sign of an open heart and a sign, too, that the accumulation of material possessions is far outweighed by 'the bargain' of heaven.

> In Alms regard thy means and others' merit.
> Think heav'n a better bargain, than to give
> Only thy single market-money for it.
> Join hands with God to make a man to live.
> Give to all something; to a good poor man,
> Till thou change names, and be where he began.
>
> ('Perirrhanterium', ll. 373–8)

'Join hands with God to make a man to live.' Herbert describes material charity as a form of co-creation whereby we join with God to offer new life. As the next stanza of the poem shows, such giving is actually a form of honouring God by recognising and honouring the image of God in the human person.

> Man is God's image; but a poor man is
> Christ's stamp to boot: both images regard.

The poor are 'Christ's stamp': nothing and no one is too lowly for the priest to notice and to care for. The priest should deal directly with children. 'If the Parson were ashamed of particularizing in these things, he is not fit to be a Parson' (Chapter XIV). Interestingly, the reformed vision of priesthood in the Catholic Reformation made many of the same points concerning priestly service, for example in the requirement of the Jesuit *Constitutions* that even the solemnly professed senior priests should give time to catechising children. Equally the priest must never hesitate to enter the very poorest cottage 'For both God is there also, and those for whom God died'.

Spiritual Guidance

What might be referred to these days as 'spiritual ministry' is a vital part of the vocation of service that Herbert describes. As well as teacher and leader of worship, the parson in Herbert's writings is a spiritual guide to individuals as well as to the whole community. Before all else he 'digested all the points of consolation' (Chapter XV 'The Parson Comforting'). The priest seeks to alleviate scruples particularly when advising people about their life of prayer, not least the problem of distractions especially during additional prayer done out of generosity of spirit rather than duty.

> God knows the occasion as well as he, and he is a gracious Father, who more accepts a common course of devotion than dislikes an occasional interruption. And of this he is so to assure himself as to admit no scruple, but to go on as cheerfully as if he had not been interrupted. By this it is evident that the distinction [made by the priest] is of singular use and comfort, especially to pious minds, which are ever tender and delicate.
>
> (Chapter XXXI 'The Parson in Liberty')

In general the priest is to attend to the spiritual state of his parishioners, responding to each according to their need. Rather as St Ignatius Loyola, in his *Spiritual Exercises* (numbers 1–20), offers advice to retreat-givers about how to teach spiritual discernment to retreatants, Herbert advises the parson to note the spiritual 'movements' within his parishioners and to react appropriately. So the priest is to advise vigilance to people who seem rather untroubled spiritually yet he is to fortify and strengthen those who are tempted.

A *Spirituality of Service*

Now the parson having a spiritual judgment, according as
he discovers any of his flock to be in one or the other state
[peaceable or 'military' – tempted], so he applies himself to
them. Those that he finds in a peaceable state, he adviseth
to be very vigilant, and not to let go the reins as soon as the
horse goes easy . . .Those that the parson finds in a military
state, he fortifies and strengthens with his utmost skill . . .

(Chapter XXXIV 'The Parson's Dexterity
in Applying of Remedies')

Herbert is very much in the tradition of the Prayer Book as well
as of the other Caroline divines, such as Jeremy Taylor, when he
recommends 'particular confession' as a comfort and remedy to
those who are afflicted in any way.

Besides this, in his visiting the sick, or otherwise afflicted, he
followeth the Church's counsel, namely, in persuading them
to particular confession, labouring to make them understand the great good of this ancient and pious ordinance.

(Chapter XV)

Individual confession was to be less narrowly focused on the
power of absolution than it was in the Roman Catholic tradition
and more broadly focused on guidance. Thus in the 1562 (and
1662) *Book of Common Prayer*, one of the exhortations for Communion days suggests that those with unquiet consciences should
seek not merely absolution but also 'ghostly counsel and advice'.
Bishop Jeremy Taylor linked spiritual guidance to confession in
his *Ductor Dubitantium*. So did Francis White in his 1625 *A Reply to
the Jesuit Fisher*. 'The true ends of private confession are these
which follow: First, to inform, instruct and counsel Christian
people . . .'. In other words, absolution did not come first. The

1634 Irish Canons suggest the same dynamic: 'Finding themselves either extreme dull or much troubled in mind, they do resort unto God's ministers to receive from them as well advice and counsel for the quickening of their dead hearts and the subduing of those corruptions whereunto they have been subject as the benefit of Absolution'.

Spiritual guidance (or 'spiritual direction') in the Anglican tradition as it is expressed by Herbert is something that should be considered ordinary rather than extraordinary. There is a thread of something we might call pastoral or spiritual conversation that runs throughout the whole of *The Country Parson*. This takes place not only in church or on religious occasions but while the priest is entertaining in his own house (Chapter VIII) or visiting people's homes and on the occasions of their everyday work (Chapter XIV). The priest's household is to share in this ministry of spiritual conversation.

> And when they go abroad, his wife among her neighbours is the beginner of good discourses, his children among children, his servants among other servants; so that as in the house of those that are skilled in music, all are Musicians; so in the house of a preacher, all are preachers.
>
> (Chapter X 'The Parson in His House')

The Service of Healing

Apart from spiritual comfort and healing, Herbert shows a marked interest in physical healing. How this interest originated is uncertain. It may reflect what we know of Herbert's own history of poor health or it may have arisen from contact with country traditions of herbal remedies. Whatever the cause, physical healing is an interesting emphasis in a document on pastoral care.

Chapter XXIII 'The Parson's Completeness' offers the most extensive treatment of physical healing. This is to be one of the parson's crucial tasks in the parish. The parson is to make sure that basic medical care is provided. Preferably he or his wife is to be a physician. Indeed, earlier in Chapter X 'The Parson in His House', skill in healing is one of the three basic qualities to be hoped for in a priest's wife. Even the priest's children are to have a modest healing role at least as visitors of the sick. Herbert lists other alternative approaches if the parson and his wife have no skill in medicine. The priest could keep a physician in his household if he can afford it or he could develop a friendly relationship with a nearby physician whom he can call into the parish when needed. Herbert shows similar concern to encourage self-help as he does in the context of charitable gifts to the poor. In Chapter XIV 'The Parson in Circuit' Herbert even suggests that the parson should pass on some medicinal knowledge to parishioners during his visits.

Herbert seeks to persuade the aspiring parish priest that herbal medicine especially is not a difficult skill to learn. He recommends certain books and also the development of a herb garden. A few examples of herbs and their uses are mentioned. Herbert argues that herbs are more natural and cheaper than drugs from an apothecary in the bigger towns. Certainly 'home-bred' herbs are to be preferred to spices and 'outlandish gums' which Herbert condemns as vanities!

Herbert is concerned to maintain the link between this concern for physical healing and spiritual ministry. Although the priest's herb garden is a 'shop' of cures to replace the city apothecary, it may also become an extension of the church building. 'In curing of any, the parson and his family use to premise prayers, for this is to cure like a parson, and this raiseth the action from the shop to the church'. If Herbert's portrayal of the organisation of the priest's lifestyle, house and family suggests echoes of monastic spirituality, the emphasis on a spirituality of herbs and healing offers other continuities with a monastic past. Shades of Brother Cadfael!

The Art of Complete and Adaptable Care

From his interest in healing, it is clear that Herbert's understanding of a spirituality of service is extremely broadly based. It expresses a sense of the completeness and adaptability of pastoral care. First the parson should seek to be involved in every aspect of the life of the parish. To some contemporary readers this may appear oppressive at first glance. However, in other ways, such a vision suggests a thoroughly modern holistic model of pastoral care. 'The country parson desires to be all to his parish, and not only a pastor, but a lawyer also, and a physician' (Chapter XXIII 'The Parson's Completeness'). As well as being teacher, leader of worship and, as we have seen, herbal doctor, the parson is to offer a modest form of legal advice. Clearly local knowledge is the bedrock of effective pastoral response and visiting is described as the most productive means.

> The country parson upon the afternoons in the weekdays, takes occasion sometimes to visit in person, now one quarter of his parish, now another. For there he shall find his flock

most naturally as they are, wallowing in the midst of their affairs. (Chapter XIV 'The Parson in Circuit')

In Herbert's mind, pastoral care must take a thorough account of individual personalities and of specific contexts. When the parson teaches he is to address concrete needs and to adopt means that speak directly to the condition of the people to whom he ministers. Country folk, for example, were deemed to be better suited to stories and sayings than to anything more abstract (e.g. Chapter VII 'The Parson Preaching'). In a country context, the priest needs to take account not only of the nature of country people ('which are thick, and heavy'!) but also of their work. The priest should place an emphasis on divine providence to counter a tendency by people to over-emphasise the natural order of things – in other words, a certain fatalism (Chapter XXX). Herbert's parson respects ancient country customs particularly those, such as processions or the blessing of lights, which have a devotional origin (Chapter XXXV 'The Parson's Condescending'). The priest should also be familiar with the everyday life of agriculture. 'He condescends even to the knowledge of tillage, and pastorage, and makes great use of them in teaching, because people by what they understand, are best led to what they understand not' (Chapter IV 'The Parson's Knowledge').

As I have suggested, some of the content and tone of *The Country Parson* appears quaint to the modern reader. Yet there are very valuable principles that stand the test of time. In particular, at the heart of Herbert's spirituality of service lies an essential respect for every kind of person even if it is cloaked in the language of the social structures and conventions of his day. A true respect for people is based on a belief that everyone, however lowly they are in human eyes, is an image of God. In a striking but probably unconscious echo of Julian of Norwich, Herbert suggests that as God is courteous to us so we are to be courteous to all people. Courtesy is shown first and foremost in responding not to stereotypes or categories but to the real person standing in front of us. A spirituality of service, therefore, must always be attentive, open, flexible, respectful and responsive.

CONCLUSION
George Herbert Today

Many people these days look to the past for spiritual wisdom, particularly in writings that are widely considered to be spiritual classics. I believe that the works of George Herbert come into this category. His poems in particular continue to be much loved by a wide readership. From a literary point of view, many scholars number Herbert among the best English poets. Certainly he is one of the most attractive examples of the literary riches of the seventeenth century. The prose work *The Country Parson* is less well known to a general readership but still finds a place in the influential series, *Classics of Western Spirituality*. It also continues to be cited by some Anglicans as a masterpiece of priestly spirituality and even a continuing model for pastoral care.

The problem, of course, with all spiritual classics is that they cannot escape their contexts. All spiritual traditions and texts of spirituality are unavoidably limited by the assumptions of particular times and places. The ways in which George Herbert's approach to spirituality is conditioned by his historical, theological and social contexts is particularly apparent in *The Country Parson*. Today's readers are often struck forcefully by Herbert's assumptions about social structures (not least the class system) and about religion that separate the text from our own times. We cannot ignore the fact that, despite the simplicity of Herbert's life in the parish (and recommendations of a simple life for parish priests), he came from an aristocratic background. It is true that he warned priests against too close an association with local landowners or nobility but Herbert's priest is still in some ways patrician and paternalistic. At the same time, Herbert's Church, while influenced by important aspects of Reformed doctrine, remained firmly unreformed in its hierarchical structures and not least in its understanding of the status of the priest.

The overwhelming impression given by *The Country Parson* is of a spirituality that is tightly ordered. The flavour of the whole is given in the telling phrase near the beginning of the book: 'A pastor is the deputy of Christ, for the reducing of man to the obedience of God'. The orderly life of the priest and his household, the right ordering of the church building, the good order of the parishioners, the maintenance of the proper order of society and of the state are no doubt capable of being seen as perfectly acceptable, if rather quaint, reflections of divine order. However, they also give the impression of a spirituality that is not merely balanced in a Benedictine sense but also controlled, controlling and deeply institutional.

Herbert's country parson operates within a fixed social order and a religious elite. As a result the priest exists in an ambiguous relationship with his parish. On the one hand he is to mix freely with parishioners, to eat with them on occasion or to entertain them in his own house. He is to view friendliness as a pastoral instrument. Yet the boundaries remain. The priest is socially removed from the rest of the village. He has an exclusive role in leading worship, in dispensing sacraments and in the key aspects of pastoral care. Herbert does not suggest a collaborative model of life and work except, in a limited way, in relation to the priest's wife and household. Hardly surprisingly, Herbert's model of pastoral care is also very masculine in an old-fashioned sense. Herbert's priest is a person of power, free standing and autonomous. His comments about the primacy of celibacy as well as about marriage and women reveal what today would be thought of as thoroughly patriarchal attitudes. The parson and his household, however modestly they live and behave, are people with servants, with financial means and with knowledge. Their role in relationship to parishioners is essentially parental. Even the parson's children and servants are drawn into this magic circle as dispensers of charity and spiritual wisdom to others.

The question that confronts any contemporary reader of all spiritual classics concerns the limits of their usefulness. In specific terms, can Herbert's spirituality be redeemed for our own age? Is there a middle way between consigning outdated texts to the rubbish heap (or to the antiquarian's bookshelf) and simply picking out the parts we like (ignoring context or the structure of the whole text) and discarding the rest? I believe that there is but we cannot be naïve about the usefulness of historical texts for our contemporary spiritual quest. We must begin by honestly acknowledging that to call a text a 'classic' does not place it on a level where it is beyond criticism. In fact, we can only read a text through the eyes of our own assumptions, values and even prejudices. We also have contexts from which we cannot escape nor should we wish to escape. Consequently, there needs to be a two-way conversation between the contemporary reader and a text from another age. In this conversation the wisdom of the text is free to challenge us, even in its strangeness, and yet we are also free to address questions to the text that arise from our own concerns and values. We may actually find meaning in the text that was unavailable to an earlier generation – and indeed may not have occurred to the original author.

So how is Herbert's spirituality still accessible to us? I believe that the most important thing is to place the poems of *The Temple* alongside *The Country Parson* when we consider the richness and potential of Herbert's spiritual vision. On its own, *The Country Parson* hardly suggests that priests share the same spiritual concerns as everyone else. The approach of the prose treatise is more austerely didactic than the poetry. Taken on its own, the emotional reticence of the text can serve to emphasise detachment both in pastoral care and in personal spirituality. The honest self-exposure and spiritual depth of *The Temple* right the balance by revealing that passion and engagement also lay at the heart of Herbert's life and ministry. In a sense, modern readers who seek to tap Herbert's spiritual wisdom do best to read the prose work from the perspective of the poems rather than the other way round.

The use of poetry itself was also a means of communicating certain values. Subjectively, Herbert understood the writing of poetry to be a form of prayer and many of the poems of the central part of *The Temple* are in the form of familiar conversations with God or Christ. As a means of teaching, poetry does not have as its primary aim the communication of information about faith or of instructions for a moral or spiritual life. Compared to the language of *The Country Parson*, the language of Herbert's poetry has an evocative quality that more readily touches the emotions. It also has a particular capacity to unlock the imagination. Poetry is more capable of speaking of the mysterious, ambiguous and complex nature of faith. It is less able to offer a complete set of directions for determining the spiritual life. Indeed, poetry suggests that spirituality is too complex a matter to be reduced to rules of life or to carefully structured techniques. The value of Herbert's poetry as spiritual wisdom, therefore, (and probably its conscious purpose) is to touch the reader in a more intimate way than the prose treatise and to provoke a deeper and more complex response.

Herbert and his circle in the Church believed in the important relationship between beauty and holiness. The aesthetic power and imagery of the poetry makes this connection real for the reader even at an unconscious level. Our postmodern world, and the spiritual climate that it encourages, is much less happy with dogma, complex definitions or rules than was the case in the past. People desire something more intimate, personal and immediate – which may be described as communion with the Absolute, the Transcendent or God. Sadly institutional Christianity has become a religion of words – or at least tends to reduce words to mere instruments of description and rational analysis. As words go, the allusive quality of poetry touches our imaginations rather than our intellect. Herbert appreciated that words must in the end give way to silence in the face of Mystery. They are always at the service of wonder. With art, music and ritual, poetry has a special power to transport us to the edge of contemplation and of mystical awareness. There are a number of other features of Herbert's spirituality that continue to offer valuable material for contemporary reflection. Spirituality does not merely consist of practices or activities but offers a way of approaching life as a whole. Even *The Country Parson* suggests that whatever is imparted to other people by way of teaching and guidance must be drawn from personal experience and from values that are lived out. The spiritual journey needs a balance between a degree of objectivity and passionate engagement. Some of the ideals presented in *The Country Parson* are in the classic spiritual tradition. However, the objectivity and detachment of the text may appear rather soulless. It is the passionate engagement and vulnerability of the poems that has the greater capacity to touch people. True spiritual wisdom and growth will touch the human and spiritual depths in ways that are challenging and painful. In other words, transformation involves struggle and the poetry is full of it. Pastoral care includes both adult education and spiritual formation. For example, Herbert spends a great deal of *The Country Parson* writing about the communication of adequate knowledge to parishioners both in terms of doctrine and of spiritual discernment. Yet, as we have seen, his poetry also suggests that there is a form of spiritual 'knowledge' to be found in aesthetic appreciation and the love of beauty that goes beyond purely conceptual thinking.

We cannot avoid the fact that the spiritual values George Herbert proposes are based on life in the Christian Church and participation in Christian worship. While this in itself does not make Herbert's spirituality inaccessible to today's readers it certainly appears to limit its appeal to a broader range of spiritual seekers. Equally, even within a Church context, the strong emphasis on the centrality of a single set form of liturgy, the *Book of Common Prayer*, would seem to distance Herbert's perspectives rather sharply from many contemporary Christians. We cannot bypass these questions. Herbert's world *is* distant from our own. Yet not everything in his writings is strange and distant. His poetry in particular continues to attract at least in part because it so honestly and authentically portrays the nature of spiritual struggle in images that transcend the boundaries of the Church. Equally, for the contemporary Christian, Herbert reminds us that spirituality is not purely a matter for individuals in isolation but concerns the nurturing of a community of faith, worship and charity.

Taken as a whole, the best of Herbert's spirituality describes a way of living and a network of relationships rather than a set of abstract theories. His spirituality concerns all aspects of human life, not simply the obviously 'religious' dimensions. In contemporary terms this would be described as holistic. Consequently many of the spiritual values that emerge from Herbert's writings continue to be accessible to people in different times and circumstances. Herbert's writings offer spiritual wisdom because he understood and evoked the depths of the human heart with insight and sensitivity.

FURTHER READING

The following are modern editions of *The Temple* and *The Country Parson*:

John N. Hall (ed.), *George Herbert – The Country Parson, The Temple*, Classics of Western Spirituality (New York: Paulist Press, 1981).

Louis L. Martz (ed.), *George Herbert and Henry Vaughan*, The Oxford Authors (Oxford/New York: Oxford University Press, 1986).

Ann Pasternak Slater (ed.), *George Herbert: The Complete English Works*, Everyman's Library (London: David Campbell Publishers, 1995).

The classic seventeenth-century *The Life of Mr. George Herbert* by Isaak Walton appears as Appendix 3 of the edition of Herbert's works by Ann Pasternak Slater (see above).

For a general introduction to the Anglican spiritual tradition see A. M. Allchin, 'Anglican Spirituality' in Stephen Sykes and John Booty (eds.), *The Study of Anglicanism* (London: SPCK/Minneapolis: Fortress Press, 1988). For a more focused study of the role of poetry in Anglican spirituality, see William Countryman, *Spirituality and Poetic Imagination: The Anglican Tradition*, Traditions of Christian Spirituality (London: Darton, Longman & Todd/New York: Orbis Books, 1999). For a brief introduction to Herbert's spirituality through his poetry, see Kenneth Mason, *George Herbert, Priest and Poet* (Oxford: SLG Press, Convent of the Incarnation, Fairacres, Oxford, 1983).

The following is a small selection of scholarly studies about George Herbert, his poetry, theology and spirituality.

Elizabeth Clarke, *Theory and Theology in George Herbert's Poetry: 'Divinitie, and Poesie, Met'* (Oxford: Clarendon Press, 1997)

Arthur L. Clements, *Poetry of Contemplation: John Donne, George*

Herbert, Henry Vaughan and the Modern Period (New York: State University of New York Press, 1990).

Richard Strier, *Love Known: Theology and Experience in George Herbert's Poetry* (Chicago: University of Chicago Press, 1986).

J.H. Summers, *George Herbert: His Religion and Art*, Medieval and Renaissance Texts and Studies (Binghampton, New York, 1981).

Gene E. Veith, *Reformation Spirituality: The Religion of George Herbert* (London & Toronto: Associated University Presses, 1985).